D0729261

Acclaim for
Memoir of a Fascist Childhood:

'This book is compelling and moving. You can get books that tell you more facts about Fascism. But nothing else offers the colour and the texture of the times and the people'
New Statesman and Society

'Trevor Grundy's survival is remarkable. And his book is salutary, because it is often funny and tells effectively of Fascism as a farce'
Nicholas Mosley, *Saturday Telegraph*

'[Grundy's] self-deprecation and honesty are admirable. Anyone who has had a simple, passionate, but troubled mother will warm to the author's struggle to rescue himself without disowning her . . . The book is not only a social document about early post-war Britain: it is also about a domestic tragi-comedy.
The book is history from the view of the small man. Let the big men take lessons from him in frankness and verve.'
Hampstead and Highgate Express

'Compelling'
Evening Standard

'The value of Grundy's memoir is that it views it from the bottom up, offering an unusual glimpse into the twilight world of working-class Fascism. This is a brave and, despite the moments of bizarre humour, an upsetting work'
Independent

'*Memoir of a Fascist Childhood* is a salutary reminder that ordinary people – star-struck women, spellbound children – were affected by what, for Mosley's languid friends, often seemed like an upper-class game'
Guardian

'Fascinating and painfully honest.'
Daily Telegraph

'This is the true story of British Fascism. Little lives, ruined by hate and by the desire to blame someone else for their fate and their failings.'
Sunday Independent

MEMOIR OF A FASCIST CHILDHOOD

Trevor Grundy was born in 1940. He spent his childhood in London, worked for many years as a journalist in Africa and now lives in Edinburgh.

Memoir of a Fascist Childhood

Trevor Grundy

ARROW

Published in the United Kingdom in 1999 by Arrow Books

1 3 5 7 9 10 8 6 4 2

Copyright © Trevor Grundy 1998

The right of Trevor Grundy to be identified as the author
of this work has been asserted by him in accordance
with the Copyright, Designs and Patents Act, 1988

First published in the United Kingdom in 1998 by William Heinemann

Arrow Books Limited
Random House UK Limited
20 Vauxhall Bridge Road, London SW1V 2SA

Random House Australia (Pty) Limited
20 Alfred Street, Milsons Point, Sydney, New South Wales 2061, Australia

Random House New Zealand Limited
18 Poland Road, Glenfield, Auckland 10, New Zealand

Random House South Africa (Pty) Limited
Endulini, 5a Jubilee Road, Parktown 2193, South Africa

Random House UK Limited Reg. No. 954009

A CIP catalogue record for this book is available from the British Library

Papers used by Random House UK Limited
are natural, recyclable products made from wood grown in
sustainable forests. The manufacturing processes conform to
the environmental regulations of the country of origin

Printed and bound in Great Britain by
Cox & Wyman Ltd, Reading, Berkshire

ISBN 0 09 927179 6

For Jane

If you don't stay bitter
and angry for too long
and have the courage to go back
you will discover that the autumn smoke
writes different more hopeful messages
in the high skies of the old country.

Charles Mungoshi (1975)

Contents

Prologue	1
Chapter 1	8
Chapter 2	36
Chapter 3	61
Chapter 4	74
Chapter 5	90
Chapter 6	106
Chapter 7	122
Chapter 8	151
Chapter 9	170
Chapter 10	196
Epilogue	201

Prologue

My father's body lay in the funeral parlour at Rayner's Lane a bit longer than is usual, as he died just before the Easter weekend of 1991. The day after his death I flew to London from Zimbabwe and the following morning I arrived on the doorstep of his council flat in Rayner's Lane. My stepmother, Peggy, opened the door, which had a brass name-plate on it. It was the first thing you saw when we lived at 40 Blandford Square, Marylebone and it read: 'S. Grundy. Photographer.'

Peggy stood back when she saw me, like a woman about to be mugged by someone she knows. Then she took a step forward and raised her arms as though she was going to put them round me. Finally, she withdrew and put her hands firmly down by her sides like a soldier. She had been a Wren in the war. My father had laughed at her, saying she'd been doubly stupid – serving the Jews *and* Winston Churchill.

'Am I pleased to see you, Trevor Grundy. I wondered if you'd ever come.' She looked at me carefully. 'I'm sorry but for a moment, in that light, you looked just like your dad.'

My father was in his eighty-fourth year when he died of heart failure. On the Saturday morning I went to say goodbye to him.

The funeral assistant was indifferently efficient. He removed the lid of the coffin before I went into the room, which was decorated

1

with spring flowers in baskets and pots. There were lots of daffodils, my father's favourite flower. I was with him only two or three minutes. I wasn't able to kiss his face, though I felt for a moment that I wanted to. I said softly, like a prayer before his shiny black coffin: 'I did try and love you, Dad.'

The following Tuesday at the crematorium we were welcomed by the young Australian vicar who was finishing a three-year secondment at a church close to Rayner's Lane. 'Good morning, Peggy, how are you? And this, of course must be Jane, Trevor's wife. There's a couple of your dad's old friends inside the church, Trevor,' said the vicar, 'friends of yours, too, I believe.'

James and Peter had telephoned to say they'd be there. 'For old times' sake, old member of Union Movement and all that,' James said. 'On behalf of Friends of Mosley. Your dad used to come to the annual dinners right up until the end. Lady Mosley still gets across from Paris. Alexander sometimes brings her.'

Most people called him Jimmy, but I had called him James from the day I'd met him, when I was eleven in 1951 and he was in his late teens. James had been a bit in love with my sister, Lovene, like most of the other young men of his generation in the Mosley movement.

The chapel could hold a hundred people. There were seven of us, eight with the vicar. No order of service had been printed and there were no hymns, but the vicar had been told a little about my father when he had come to see us at the flat.

'Tell me about your dad,' he'd said. 'I never had the pleasure of meeting him, so we get someone close to him to recall what he was like, what he most liked doing, and then I read out a bit during the service, which, I hope, gives the impression that I really knew him.'

In the chapel on that cold Tuesday morning he read: 'Sidney Grundy was almost eighty-four when he died, a good man with a loving family. He was much loved by his wife, Peggy, his son Trevor and his wife, Jane, and Benjamin, who is one of Lovene's sons. Lovene is in America and unfortunately couldn't get across.

'Mr Grundy was born in January 1908, and Trevor told me that when he was young it looked as if he was going to become a vicar, but for some reason he didn't end up with a dog collar around his neck. Perhaps he was lucky. I'm told Mr Grundy loved music and could play the piano beautifully. His favourite composers were Beethoven, Mozart and Wagner.' He pronounced the Wagner with a W. 'Well, each to his own, but I can't help thinking of what Mark Twain said about Wagner, that his music was better than it sounded.'

Silence met the joke.

'I'm afraid one of the biggest blows to hit the Grundy family was the sudden death of the first Mrs Grundy in 1970. Trevor's and Lovene's mother died very suddenly and tragically but we don't have to go into that today. Mr Grundy was an extremely fortunate man because he married again and enjoyed more than twenty years with his second wife, Peggy, his cousin and a lady who loved her husband very much and looked after him superbly during his last years when he was ill.'

Peggy had her head down.

'I think Mr Grundy must have earned a lot of respect during his life and Trevor has told me that when he was a London taxi driver he used to volunteer to take disabled children to Brighton for the day. He was adored by his grandsons who thought the world of him.'

I thought: 'Without this well-meaning Australian man of God my father would just slip away.'

'In the name of the Father and of the Son and of the Holy Ghost.' We bowed our heads and I found my thoughts wandering to another time, another death, another father.

Eleven years earlier, Mosley's death in Paris had intruded abruptly on my life in Zimbabwe. Sir Oswald Mosley was eighty-four when he died at his home outside Paris, in a house called Le Temple de la Gloire, which had been built in 1800 for General Moreau, who was one of Napoleon's marshals.

He had died at almost the same time as a mentally disturbed American, with a copy of Salinger's *The Catcher in the Rye* under his arm, killed John Lennon. I searched *Time* and *Newsweek* magazines which carried front page pictures of Lennon and eventually found a tiny obituary on Mosley in *Time*, which quoted one of his sons, the novelist Nicholas Mosley: 'I see clearly that while the right hand dealt with grandiose ideas and glory, the left hand let the rats out of the sewer.'

It took me close on a decade to gather any further information about Sir Oswald's funeral. I had written to several people who might have been invited but no one replied. One day in 1990, out of the blue I received a letter with a Winchester postmark. It was unsigned and contained the briefest description of the formal event. I have no idea why the letter was sent like some secret communiqué, but the Mosley movement bred secrecy.

The service had been held at the crematorium on the hilltop above the famous Père Lachaise cemetery, which also contains Oscar Wilde and Jim Morrison of The Doors. There was no religious leader but there wasn't any chance of Sir Oswald Mosley just slipping away. It was a freezing day and there was nothing for the congregation to do but stand around. There were no hymns to sing, no versicles to respond to, and no prayers to say 'amen' to. Although there were over two hundred people at the service, only three or four of Mosley's former Fascists had been invited. One of them was a Welsh schoolteacher named Jeffrey Hamm.

A grand professional choir, hired from a local opera company, sang excerpts from Verdi's *Requiem*, the Sanctus and Agnus Dei from the plainsong Requiem Mass, some bits of Bach, César Franck, Mozart's *Ave Verum*, Handel's Hallelujah chorus and finished with a virtuoso organ recital of Handel's air to the song 'Here the conquering hero comes' from *Judas Maccabaeus*.

Between the musical items there were readings – by three of Mosley's sons, Nicholas, Max and Michael, and other friends – of extracts from Goethe, Nietzsche, Paul Valéry and Swinburne.

I imagined the speeches, the choir, the music, especially 'Here the conquering hero comes' which, ironically, was dedicated to one of the great folk heroes of the Jews. Mosley's funeral, like one of his great orations at the Albert Hall or Olympia in the 1930s, must have reached a crescendo of sound and colour, reminding some of the onlookers of the tragic squandering of his talent.

A hand touched my shoulder and brought me back to the present of my own father's funeral service. Peter whispered, 'Trev, if you want one of us to take the vicar outside for a moment you can do *the* salute over the coffin. It's often done at funerals of old members. It'll only take a second and the vicar wouldn't see.'

I must have made some gesture of sympathy and understanding because James smiled at me and reached across and patted my shoulder.

The vicar continued: 'Trevor told me that before the service ends today he'd like to say a few words. When I met Trevor last week for the first time he said he thought the words St Paul spoke to the Corinthians were the most beautiful he'd ever read, so it's appropriate he should read them at the funeral of his sadly missed father.'

My hands were shaking. When I found the right section I looked at Peggy. 'I don't have much to say because the vicar has already said most of it. I want to try and remember the good things about my father, just as you do.'

I felt the eyes of James and Peter bore into me. The last time they had heard me speak was at Trafalgar Square, shortly after my seventeenth birthday.

'St Paul was talking to his disciples about what really matters.' I paused for a moment. ' "Though I speak with the tongues of men and of angels, and have not charity, I am become as sounding brass, or a tinkling cymbal. And though I have the gift of prophecy, and understand all mysteries, and all knowledge; and though I have all faith, so that I could remove mountains, and have not charity, I am nothing. And though I bestow all my goods to feed the poor; and though I give my body to be burned, and have not charity, it profiteth me nothing." '

I took a deep breath and looked up to see the vicar smiling brightly to encourage me. I read slowly. ' "When I was a child, I spake as a child, I understood as a child, I thought as a child, but when I became a man, I put away childish things. For now we see through a glass,

5

darkly; but then face to face: now I know in part; but then shall I know even as also I am known. And now abide faith, hope, charity, these three: but the greatest of these is charity."'

As we left the chapel, the vicar smiled at me and shook my hand. 'Well done,' he said. 'You read that beautifully.'

James frowned at me and asked, 'Why did you read a piece which gave the impression that your father was involved in something childish?'

A three-course pub lunch awaited us after the service.

'Your dad left money for everything,' Peggy said. 'He left it in envelopes marked "funeral", "the car", "lunch", "drinks".'

James and Peter collared me. 'Never thought we'd see you drinking non-alcoholic beer. I said to Peter this morning, well, if we're going to see Trev Grundy it's going to turn into a right old piss-up, but I don't suppose now is the right time.

'We're a respectable lot now, you know, Trev, we're company directors. I'm sure you know that Max is one of the best-known men in the motor racing industry. Still married to Jean. And Alexander is a publisher in France and neither has anything to do with politics, right-wing or left-wing, though Max did try to get selected as a Conservative MP, can you imagine?

'Every year, the Friends of Mosley have a dinner near Victoria. Alexander sometimes brings Lady Mosley across. She's frail and stone deaf but still beautiful and dignified and Alexander is such a good-looking bloke, grey hair now, married to some beautiful young girl called Charlotte. He's tall and imposing like his father but he's never had anything to do with the Movement or Friends of Mosley, just sits there politely with his mother making sure she's okay.

'But whenever he's been across he asks after you and said to your father last time: "And how are Trevor and Lavinia, Mr Grundy?" Always calls her *Lavinia*. And people say: "Whatever happened to Sid Grundy's boy, the one who spoke at Trafalgar Square?" See, Trev, you're famous but you've never been back once.'

'Well, we're not going to let go of you this time, Trev. On Friday night we're going to have a bit of a do for your father at my house.' He gave me his card. It had a Bethnal Green address. 'I'm not sure how many people will turn up, probably a couple of hundred. You know what the Movement grapevine is like. It would be our way of saying goodbye to your father. There's a set of drums up in the attic and we bring them down now and again. Funnily enough, the neighbours don't seem to mind. Secret supporters, perhaps. Well, no one has complained yet.

'Will Jane come?' James continued. 'I mean, she knows about Union Movement?'

'She knows,' I said.

In front of the two middle-aged Mosley stalwarts, I stood up as straight and tall as I could, like a new recruit on the parade ground and imagined I heard, 'Buttons need shining, hair needs cutting but under the circumstances the new recruit looks promising, sir!'

I was no new recruit, yet I feared the sound of a whistle that would make me fall into line, follow orders once more.

After the meal, James and Peter got into their car. One of them turned on a tape and I heard marching music and drums. James smiled. I thought he was going to wave at all of us but instead he looked only at me and raised his right arm in a half-salute, the sort Mosley did after the war when he was respectable, no longer a Fascist.

Without thinking, I returned the salute and caught Jane's eye. Later, I told her what I'd done and she said, 'No one knew. I thought you were just waving. Why are you so upset? It's not important. You always turn things into such a drama.'

1

My mother said at supper, as if she were starting a fairy-tale: 'If you want to know the truth, listen to what I tell you.' It was the summer of 1948 and I was eight years old.

'You were in your pram and I was pushing. Your father was walking along holding Lovene's hand when we turned the corner and there they were. The Special Branch, sitting in a car. One got out and asked, "Are you Sidney Grundy of 23 Buckingham Road, Brighton?"

'They let your father pack a few things and took him away. Before he left, he said, "Is this the right thing, Edna?" And I said to him, "We'll never betray The Leader." And they drove away with your father looking at me through the back window.'

I looked at my mother and wanted to burst with pride. Nothing could ever destroy this woman, this magnificent mother who was like a goddess. What courage when everyone else was going off to fight a Jewish war.

I had seen pictures of the men in tin hats in *Picture Post*; they were always smiling and smoking. Usually, the women were crying or waving or giving the V-sign like Mr Churchill.

My father hadn't been so stupid as to go. Churchill had organised the war to get power. Churchill was Jewish but that was a secret only a few people knew. My mother, my father, Lovene, me and, of course, The Leader.

My mother put aside her knife and fork and acted out the parts.

8

'They let your father come home after six months. I never found out why. They stood him in front of a tribunal of old men, church people. I listened from the gallery and sent out vibes so he'd be strong and not weaken. One man said, "Doesn't your conscience prick you, Mr Grundy, you safe in prison while everyone else is being bombed and everyone you went to school with fighting the Germans? Do you still object to fighting a man whose evil hordes are invading neutral countries, Mr Grundy? Neutral countries!"'

I stopped eating and stared, knowing exactly when the earthquake would occur. My mother looked at me and turned her eyes into dark brown balls. My father called it her 'Mosley look'.

'Then your father stared at me from the dock and said as loud as he could in front of all the church fuddy-duddies in Brighton: "As long as my Leader is in prison without trial, I will also stay in prison without trial!"'

She mimicked: ' "Take him away!" said the magistrate. "Take him away and lock him up until he sees sense. Next case!"' and she banged her fist on the table making the fish cakes jump. "Next case!" and she banged the table even harder. Bonnie, our wire-haired fox terrier, whom my father had bought for thirteen guineas at Phyllis Stein's Pet Shop opposite the Classic Cinema in Baker Street, wagged her tail and barked.

After we'd eaten, my mother continued: 'Two months after you were born, Trevor, in May 1940, Sir Oswald Mosley, The Leader, was arrested. And later his wife Diana, who'd just given birth to their second son, was also picked up by the police.'

When Mummy told how Max, the baby, was separated from his mother who was carted off to prison, I gripped the edge of the wooden kitchen table. I felt that Max was my brother because we were the same age. My father went to prison at almost exactly the same time as his. But Max was a bit better than me, even though he was one month younger, because his father was The Leader.

My mother said: 'Lady Mosley was feeding him when a Special Branch man came and pulled Max off her breast. They hauled her off to prison. The two boys, Max and Alexander, were left without their mother and father and had to go into a home with a nanny,' and my mother's dark eyes flashed with anger.

She told us these stories often, sometimes with very little or no emotion in her voice but usually she acted it all out with great feeling. I would try to hold Lovene's hand under the table but my beautiful, dark-haired, brown-eyed sister, who was five years older than me, pushed me away. Just before my mother turned round from the sink, Lovene mouthed the usual word which never failed to fix me to my chair: 'Weed!'

My mother told us that one night, not long after the sirens had started and people in Brighton and elsewhere were digging holes four feet deep as bomb shelters and covering them with tin roofs, the Special Branch men came again to the Grundy flat.

As she spoke, my mother touched the top of her head and with both hands patted the sides of it, like a woman about to go on stage or deliver an important charity appeal into a microphone.

'I asked them what they wanted and one of them said, "You've got to leave Brighton." "Why?" I asked. "Because you're a security risk. The Germans might invade and you could go down to the beach at night and shine a torch." "I haven't got a torch," I said. "Have you ever heard of matches?" he asked and I said, "Rubbish. Mosley told us all to do nothing to damage England, even though we're at war because of the Jews."'

We knew the story by heart but Lovene and I always behaved as if it were the first time we'd heard it.

'So the three of us left Brighton for London by train.' She leant forward with her full lower lip resting on top of her crossed hands, which were already beginning to show the small lumps and bumps that signal the start of arthritis.

'Our new neighbours in London said to me: "So where's your man?" and I said that your father was on special duties and I'd been told not to tell anyone because of the Official Secrets Act. And then I'd ask, "And where's your man?" and one of them said, "He was killed at Dunkirk." I wanted to say, "You fools, if only you'd listened to Mosley."

10

'Before he went to prison your father taught Lovene to speak a bit of German. What was it, Lovene? *Wir sind Freunde* . . . we're your friends.' She laughed. 'That was all your father could say in German, that and *Sieg heil!*'

I was two when we moved, Lovene seven and my mother thirty-five, a strange little fatherless Fascist family heading for the London Blitz. My mother said that the police found the flat for us, one room in a house, 66 Loudoun Road, midway between St John's Wood and Swiss Cottage.

Lovene attended a local primary school in the mornings and in the afternoons stayed with me while my mother went out on her own for long walks. Once or twice a week my mother would slip something sweet-tasting into my mouth when she was washing me. She told me that American friends gave her chewing gum and sometimes fruit sweets which tasted of real oranges and pears. Once I was clean, she'd stick a pink, prickly embrocation called Thermogene onto my chest, wrap sticking plaster over it and button up my shirt. It made me look overfed, even fat. She told Lovene, 'Trevor's like Uncle Rolly, he's got a weak chest. If I don't take care he'll turn into a sickly child dependant on me for the rest of his life, or die of TB like your uncle.' She always made me wear a jacket and striped tie and even when it was quite hot outside I had to wear a thick overcoat because of my supposedly weak chest.

Sometimes I watched her staring out of the window when it was raining, which was most of the time. Even then I thought her an extremely beautiful woman with her auburn hair, perfectly shaped Roman nose, dark eyes, lovely soft skin and full figure. I remember that when we went across to the shop on the opposite side of Loudoun Road, people treated her with respect. The butcher and the greengrocer let her pay 'next week', though I can't remember her ever having any money in her purse.

When I turned four I heard women in the shops say that soon the war would be over. 'Then we'll show Mr Hitler who's the boss,' laughed a big fat woman with red cheeks and blonde hair. She put her arm around my mother; I thought, 'How unusual. I've never seen anyone touch my mother.' My mother winced as if she were in pain.

'It'll be nice to have 'em back again, won't it, luv?' said the woman. My mother said nothing but pulled me along back to the flat as if I were a puppy on a lead.

At night my mother opened the door of a small wooden cupboard next to the lavatory. When we heard the planes she would wake us up and we would all squeeze into the cupboard. She put her arms around us and the three of us would make a unit, a single cuddle. The doodlebug was right overhead and we heard its whine, then silence and my mother counted: 'Nine, eight, seven, six, five, four, three, two, one and . . .'

Afterwards she told us that if you could hear the explosion you knew you were still alive. Once she explained that a very great and good man called Hitler was trying to rescue Daddy and The Leader. After Hitler won the war, both would be released. Then the Jews would be for it.

Towards the end, the bombing became so bad that a worried neighbour knocked at the door of our flat in her nightie. My mother left us alone in the cupboard.

'You shouldn't be on your own in there with two kids, missus. Your old man's out there fighting for you and yours but this is taking a risk without reason. Come down to the shelter at the end of the road, we'll fit you in.'

At the shelter, while the bombs piled onto London, my restless and frightened nine-year-old sister turned over in her top bunk and fell out onto the concrete floor. She badly split her top lip and when the Germans flew away again she was taken to Great Ormond Street Hospital.

When we went to visit her the nurse asked my mother, 'Can't you send the children away somewhere, Mrs Grundy?'

My mother said she would write to her mother and father who lived outside Newcastle, but several months later we were still at 66 Loudoun Road.

In September 1944 a letter arrived. My mother read it slowly to

12

herself and then told us to sit on the bed with her. I knew it was terribly important because on the back of the envelope there was a crown. It was from the King. She read it aloud, without a hint of drama in her voice.

Sir,

I am directed by the Secretary of State to inform you that the Restriction Order made against you under Regulation 18A of the Defence (General) Regulations, 1939, has now been revoked.

I am, Sir, Your obedient Servant

'Only a civil servant could lock you up for four years and sign himself, *Your obedient Servant*,' my mother commented. 'So your father will be home soon,' she added, gazing out of the window at the black, leafless trees.

She put the letter on the mantelpiece next to the clock and a very small picture which she had of The Leader, with his dark hair combed back and his fiercely intelligent eyes staring down a long Roman nose, just like my mother's.

My mother had shown me a picture of my father wearing a black shirt before the war. His head was turned slightly sideways, revealing a very large nose, and his hair was swept back and heavily greased in the style of the time. My mother said he had lovely pale blue eyes but that his lips were much too thin, 'Just like his Scottish schoolmarm mother's.' My father's most outstanding feature, said my mother, looking down at the small photograph which she kept in an envelope in the kitchen drawer, were his hands. 'He has the most beautiful hands and if he had been properly trained could have been a concert pianist. His father, your grandfather Grundy, was the church organist when we got married.'

Lovene and I had never seen our grandparents either on the Grundy side of the family or on my mother's side. She told us her maiden name was Maurice. She always emphasised the spelling, 'ice', she'd say, verbally underlining the three letters, 'ice not is.'

My father returned. He picked me up and looked me full in the face.

'My God, Edna,' he said, 'he's the double of Uncle Jamie.' I didn't know if that was a good thing or a bad thing. I hadn't met Uncle Jamie or any of our relatives.

My father put me down when Lovene came into the room. He cuddled her and kissed her face. He clearly adored her. He kept kissing the stitches in her upper lip. 'My poor, poor darling,' he said.

He proudly announced to my mother that he had given up smoking in prison: 'That's why I've put on a few pounds.' My mother said he'd soon lose them once he started working and got us somewhere decent to live.

That night I heard the bed creak and listened to them talking. I snuggled up to Lovene and whispered, 'What are they doing?' and she nudged me and said, 'Keep quiet and go to sleep. You always want to know everything.' I remember thinking that even though he was my father he had no right to be in bed with my mother, making a noise like that.

In the morning he looked through the newspapers, searching for a job. Occasionally, while he was reading, he would pull me towards him without looking up and I sat on his knee. 'You don't really know who I am, do you?' he said. 'But I've been away most of your life, haven't I, so we'll have to get to know each other all over again.'

Not long after that the rows started. Angry words were exchanged in the tiny kitchen, but at lunch- or suppertime they would pretend that nothing had happened. My mother said that Lovene and I were too sensitive and that all mothers and fathers had rows. 'Trouble is, you're both Pisces. You were both born in March and you're both fish swimming in opposite directions. It's a watery sign and Pisceans usually end up being drunks.'

Lovene and I would find the stars column in the *Evening News*, *Evening Standard* or the *Star* and look for the double fish sign. It always said that we were nice people to know but too easily influenced by those around us. I said to Lovene: 'I'll never drink beer like Daddy because Mummy says I'll be a drunkard like the man downstairs.'

On Victory Day every child in Loudoun Road and the adjoining area was invited to a large street party. Tables were set up in the middle of the road and there were bottles of lemonade, red, white and blue cakes, pictures of Mr Churchill doing the V-sign and at least six Union Jacks hanging from shops opposite our house. A dozen or so yards from the table was a large bonfire and on it a stuffed effigy of a man with a moustache and a lank lock of hair falling over one side of his forehead. I had seen this man sitting next to the potatoes and cabbages in the greengrocer's shop and women coming and going said, 'Morning, Adolf! Not feeling much like bombing us today, are we?'

The day before Victory Day my parents had a gigantic row. Lovene and I stood out on the landing, listening to the shouting.

'They'll stick a Union Jack on his head and tell him lies about Hitler!' screamed my mother. 'What did you go to prison for if you're letting your only son be paraded in front of a burning Hitler?'

My father opened the flat door and told us to come inside. They both calmed down. They looked like Catherine Wheels that had burnt out and stopped spinning. As if officially to end the row my mother made a cup of tea and then sat staring into space. My father went out to buy an evening newspaper and Lovene and I played another instalment of a radio programme called *The Way to the Stars*. I was an RAF hero and Lovene was my girlfriend. Then we took it in turns to scrape the condensed milk tin and my mother said that we would both die of tin poisoning. My future was bleak. I'd become a drunk unless I was careful or suffer a slow, lingering death from tin poisoning.

On the morning of the celebration my father took me to the washbasin and combed my hair flat against my head, with a parting on the right which some of the kids in Loudoun Road said was the girl's side. He put me into a grey shirt and shorts and knotted my tie. At eleven o'clock he took me downstairs into the road and we joined a party of boys my own age. A large woman with an enormous bust put her arm around my shoulders and pulled me towards her. 'You from sixty-six, are you, luvvie?' She put a paper Union Jack shaped like an upside-down ship on my head and someone took a photograph. My father walked away but turned several times to check

15

that I was all right. Within a few minutes, I was standing on my own holding a large sticky bun and a mug full of lemonade.

'Where's your sister then, luvvie. What's her name again? Something French?'

'Levy something,' said a man lifting an accordion from the back seat of a small car. 'I think your dad must have made a few lady friends in France during the war to come up with a name like that.' They laughed and I remembered that my mother hadn't said a word about Lovene attending the Victory Day parade. I wondered if it was only for boys but no, there were plenty of girls of Lovene's age in the street that day.

After our lemonade and cakes the vicar said that we were gathered together on this wonderful sunny day in 1945 to celebrate the end of the war and to praise God for making sure that good had once again triumphed over evil. He turned to the man with the accordion and said, 'I think now.'

The bonfire was lit and a vast orange flame leapt into the air and started to lick the face of the man with the moustache, who crackled, slumped and exploded. After a while he disappeared, to the cheers of the children and the roars of approval from mums and dads, the greengrocer, the butcher, the postman and a couple of policemen, who looked old and tired in their dark blue uniforms and helmets. The vicar beamed at the man with the accordion and later pretended to conduct an orchestra. Everyone was singing but I sat quite silent and on my own.

> Hitler has only got one ball
> Goering has got one very small
> Himmler has something similar
> But poor old Goebbels has no balls at all.

I laughed and clapped with everyone else and then the Union Jack cake was cut. I kept the icing for Lovene in my pocket and told myself to remember the words of the song because I was good at that. I would sing the song to my mother when I got back home.

That would cheer her up.

In 1946 my father got a job with Kodak and was responsible for packing and loading films and photographic paper into lorries.

We left the flat in Loudoun Road. My father signed a lease with the London North Eastern Railways and became the landlord of a tall, badly bombed Victorian house in Blandford Square, behind Marylebone Station. Although he did not own the house, once it was repaired – at his expense – he could make money by letting flats. My mother was overjoyed when told she would be the landlady. She emphasised the word *lady* in the same way she always emphasised the word *Sir* when she spoke about Mosley.

Our house, number forty, was large. It consisted of a basement, ground floor and three storeys above that. The front of the house looked upon what had once been a perfectly proportioned square, now spoilt by a tall railway building. At the end of the square there was a brick wall which looked onto the back of Marylebone Station. Immediately opposite, in Harewood Avenue, was St Edward's Convent, a grey-and-black stone building with towers and mysterious windows. From the outside it looked like a castle for ladies and their knights, rather than a home for nuns and their pretty-faced but undernourished-looking novices.

Our flat occupied the ground floor of the house and consisted of a fairly large 'front room', which doubled up as a bedroom for my parents. When I was a child, until about the age of eleven, I slept in a single bed in the corner of that room. A thin wooden partition divided the front room from my sister's room, with its bed, wardrobe, table, record player and books – mainly about Vincent Van Gogh, the Impressionists and great musicians. Later, I was moved downstairs into the cold and damp basement. My parents said it wasn't right that I should sleep in their room and so a small room was whitewashed, a bed was installed along with a table and chair where I could do my homework. In the summer it was cool, like sitting inside a refrigerator; in winter, it was deathly cold and I'd stay upstairs in the front room after school until it was bedtime, when I descended into the dungeon of the house.

Two flights of stairs up from our flat was the only bathroom in the house. Everyone used it. To get hot water you put pennies in a gas meter. Out of a large copper geyser flowed boiling water, until the money ran out and then it went icy cold. All the water pipes were outside the house and they usually froze over at Christmas time. Plumbers came to the house and seemed to take it over for days on end. With their blowlamps and tools they made the water unfreeze and run again, so that the lavatory could flush and baths be run once more. And if that failed, the residents of number forty, with many others from Blandford Square, could be seen walking off to Seymour Place, towels under arms, heading for the public baths at the council swimming pool.

By the time we moved to Marylebone, the word 'square' was inappropriate because three sides of the square had been amputated to make way for the station. My father spotted a picture of Blandford Square, a crayon drawing, in a book called *Great Houses of London*. It delighted my mother, the land*lady*. My father told us that between 1860 and 1865 a woman called Mary Ann Evans, better known as the novelist George Eliot, had lived at 16 Blandford square. Artists and writers, he assured us, had lived in and around the square until the station had been constructed, when they'd deserted the area for the more salubrious air of Hampstead and Highgate.

Behind Blandford Square was Sherborne Place, a maze of tiny houses converted into flats, where, my mother said, the 'poor people' lived. Proudly, she told us that in its glory Blandford Square had been protected from the eyes of the poor and envious by high, locked gates and only those rich enough to own houses in the square were allowed keys. The 'fancy people' lived in Blandford Square and their coachmen, servants and families lived in Sherborne Place. People who lived in 'squares' would one day support The Leader, my mother said, but people who lived in 'places' were nearly always Communists.

At number thirty-three, Mr and Mrs Adams lived with their son Timothy, who was six months younger than me. He never stopped blinking. He was my first friend in Blandford Square and he was always being punished for something or other. Sometimes Tim wasn't allowed out of the house for days. He'd lean out of the top-flat window, wave and giggle. Then he'd be pulled back inside by his father, the window went down and the curtains closed.

My parents bought me a second-hand two-wheeler bicycle. I sat on it and pedalled carefully in case I wobbled, fell off and was called *Weed* by my sister. Tim waved frantically when he saw me. Once he opened the window half-way and shouted: 'I can come out to-morrow.' But as fast as it opened it closed again. I kept my eyes set straight ahead of me because I knew Mr Adams was watching.

When Tim was allowed out of the house we would go and play football with a tennis ball in Harewood Avenue, using the doors of the convent as goalposts. When we kicked the ball over the smoke-blackened stone wall a pretty young Irish nun would come to the gate, look through the grille and smile and frown at the same time. 'This is the last time I'm giving you your ball back today, now do you hear me, you naughty boys!'

Most Saturday mornings Tim and I went by bus to Swiss Cottage Odeon. For sixpence we watched *Tom Mix*, saw newsreels about the last days of the Germans and a vast range of cartoons. Before the show, we sang the Odeon Saturday Morning Club song, which came up on the screen after the organist disappeared into the bowels of the earth. A white ball bounced over each word and we yelled out:

> *We come along on Saturday morning*
> *Greeting everybody with a smile.*
> *We come along on Saturday morning*
> *Knowing it's well worthwhile.*
> *As members of the Odeon we all intend to be*
> *Good citizens when we grow up*
> *And champions of the Free.*

At the end of the show Tim and I stood to attention to stop the other children pushing past us, children who did not want to waste time standing up for the King. My mother said the King was there to protect people from Communists and Jews.

One Saturday morning before lunch Tim and I went to Bell Street. He found a very old Bible on one of the stalls. Tim believed that anything old must be expensive. He opened it at Kings I and pointed at an illustration. 'She looks like your mother.'

The colourful picture showed a dark woman in a shawl. Standing next to her in the kitchen was a small boy who looked ill. Next to the mother and son was a tall shining man in white with a long grey beard. His name was Elijah.

'A very great prophet,' I told Tim, who said he had never heard of Elijah. 'Don't you know about the miracle at Zarephath?' I asked. My mother had told me about it and said that if I knew the Bible I couldn't go wrong in life.

I said to Tim, 'She looks a bit like her but not really. Everyone in the Bible is Jewish and my mother isn't Jewish.' Then I added before we went our separate ways, 'And she'd be furious if she knew you'd said that. Furious!'

In 1946 my parents decided to send me to school at St Paul's, where Lovene was in the top class. At my interview I met Mr Walker, the school headmaster, who was a giant of a man with short iron-grey hair. He wore a tan-coloured Harris tweed jacket and trousers which made him look like a mountain bear.

His assistant, Mr Simon, was a sharp-faced man who rarely smiled. He wore a sports jacket, a red tie and circular, wire-rimmed spectacles, which clung to the end of his nose. During the interview he told my mother that he was well-qualified to teach at a grammar school but didn't want to. 'I want to teach the children of the working class.'

Mr Simon said that he liked Mr Attlee, the Labour Prime Minister, but his personal heroes were a man called Morrison and another called Bevan, who came from Wales. My mother kept remarkably quiet and listened to him with a Mosley-look on her face. She told Mr Walker that she was a land*lady* in Marylebone and that her personal hero was St Paul, which made Mr Walker look at Mr Simon and grin. He asked her why and she said: 'When he found Jesus he never

20

turned back and those are the people who finally get things done in this world, Mr Simon.'

My father said he was delighted that I had got into a decent school at Swiss Cottage. But he warned me never to go to sleep on the bus because I'd get into big trouble if I ended up in Golders Green and didn't have a special passport to be there.

I made a mental note to ask Mr Simon why.

To celebrate, the four of us went to an Indian restaurant off Regent Street, called Veraswamis.

At the entrance to the restaurant was a dark wooden chair shaped like an elephant and an Indian waiter told me that if I could pick it up I could take it home with me. 'Indians are nice with kids,' said my father on the way home. 'Yes,' said my mother, 'but they'd be even nicer if they were in their own country.'

The next morning, and for the next three years, I put on my green school blazer with its red 'SP' on the breast pocket, my school cap and picked up my satchel. I turned at the end of Blandford Square and waved to my mother, who was standing on the front doorstep. She called out my name, stood to attention and flung her right arm up into the air in a full Fascist salute. I returned it. 'PJ,' she shouted, Mosley-member speak for 'Perish Judah'. I shouted it back and then ran down Harewood Avenue, past Marylebone Station, through Dorset Square and into the Abbey National entrance to Baker Street, where I joined a queue of people waiting for buses to take them to St John's Wood, Swiss Cottage, Finchley Road and Golders Green.

I often asked myself what I would do if I fell asleep on the bus and woke up in Golders Green and the conductor came up to me and said, 'Passport please, passport.'

Once the floors were repaired at 40 Blandford Square people came to see the shell of the empty flats. They were delighted to move into a house so central, so close to Baker Street, with a prestigious NW1 address and Ambassador telephone number.

A man who described himself as a colonel in the Free Polish Army moved into one flat with his effervescent French wife and grown-up daughter. Above them lived a single woman who my father said was the spitting image of the dancer Margot Fonteyn. In one half of the basement there was a Scottish woman who had a different husband for every day of the week. She played the radio very loudly and ate so much garlic the house smelt.

In the other half of the basement lived a man who my mother said was one day going to be as famous as St Paul. His name was Jeffrey Hamm. My father didn't charge Mr Hamm rent because he was one of Mosley's most loyal followers and, with other leading members of the British Union of Fascists, had been in prison on the Isle of Man right through the war. Mr Hamm was extremely tall and thin and always wore the same jacket and trousers. He was planning to form a non-political organisation for British ex-servicemen, even though he had not fought in the war. He lived with his wife, Lily, in a single room and shared an outside lavatory with the garlic-eater, but they never complained about anything.

Mr Hamm sometimes spoke to me. He said that the future was with Britain's youth and that one day I might hear the greatest man England had ever produced speak. My father said that Mosley was a great man but that he would never get anywhere in British politics because he had crossed swords with the Jews who would never forgive him. But Mr Hamm said, 'The Leader's not looking for forgiveness. We were right, Mr Grundy. We *were* right and we *are* right.'

My father told my mother that Jeffrey was wasting his life if he ever thought there would be a Mosley revival, and about this time my father started bringing home maps from the South African High Commission in Trafalgar Square. Even though he was making good money for the first time in his life, my father thought England was finished. 'There's a big world out there, Edna,' he said, 'and what's keeping us in this dump with Attlee and the Jews in control?'

One room of the house was full of photographic paper and hundreds of rolls of black-and-white film which my father sold for Kodak at the weekend to people he knew all around London. I was told not to tell anyone what was in the room. Then, after quite a short time at Kodak, my father came home one night with two Leica cameras and told my mother that his days of working for other people were over. He had a pitch at Hampton Court and would take souvenir pictures of couples reunited after the war as they walked by the Thames. 'I may as well make something out of the war.' He laughed and my mother, the land*lady*, agreed to clean out a back room downstairs for him to use as a dark-room. A prison friend had taught my father how to develop and print pictures, and now he had a brass name-plate made for the front door and a rubber stamp, which he used to smack down on the back of his prints. They both read *S. Grundy. Photographer.*

One afternoon as the school bell rang, I saw my mother standing at the gate. It was 1948 and Britain was recovering from a bitter winter during which the lake in Regent's Park had frozen over. Despite the cold, my mother was bubbling with excitement. She told me that Bill Dodds, a good-looking man with dark hair and a moustache, who was almost as tall as Mosley, had been twiddling the knobs on his powerful new radio set and had heard Hitler, speaking in German. Hitler had not killed himself in the bunker in 1945 but was alive in South Africa, or was it South America . . . Bill Dodds was not sure because there had been some static interference caused by Jewish technicians at the BBC, which had banned mention of Hitler or Mosley after the war.

She told me that we, too, were going to live in South Africa. She would show me where it was on the map when we got home. The town was called Johannesburg, which meant 'City of Gold', and the whole place was under the control of a man called Dr Malan, who had supported Hitler and was a close friend of The Leader. We were going there with the Peroni and Dodds families from West Hampstead. There was a good chance we would be joined by a famous Mosley speaker called Victor Burgess, perhaps even by Jeffrey Hamm and others who had been in prison.

'Your father has been promised a good job. It's warm. The schools are good and there are servants because most of the black people don't have jobs.'

The following morning I told my eight-year-old girlfriend Maureen that she would have to find a new boyfriend. Tears filled her eyes when I told her about South Africa. But I also told her that my mother had promised we would come straight back to England when Mosley came to power and that would be about 1950, certainly no later than 1955. By then we would be fifteen, almost old enough to get married.

But it was The Leader himself who stopped our plan to leave England and go to South Africa. One freezing night in February 1948, Jeffrey Hamm came up the stone basement stairs and knocked on the kitchen door. He had on his usual light sports jacket. My mother made him some soup and he ate it quickly with almost half a loaf of bread and margarine. He nervously pushed back his hair and sat perched on the edge of his chair. He told the Grundy family that he had some exciting news from Ireland, where Mosley had gone to live after his release from prison. Mosley was returning to Britain, he told us, to start his new political organisation. It was to be called Union Movement. Jeffrey Hamm had done much of the spadework by helping to set up bookshops which were distributing some of Mosley's pre-war books, his defence of his war position and a new book called *The Alternative*.

Jeffrey said he had heard about our plan to move to South Africa but hoped that would not happen now because Mosley needed every man, woman and child, and with a smile on his Welsh face which was probably irresistible to women, he looked at me.

I remember glancing at my parents and then at Lovene, who was thirteen and mildly interested in a new life in South Africa but not wildly enthusiastic. She said she felt sorry for the blacks in that country.

My mother leant back in her chair and rested her head. My father stood up and for some reason I thought he was going to hit Jeffrey, but he didn't. Instead he saluted him and went to a long, low oak sideboard, which he had bought at an auction for a few pounds the week before. The cupboard had several drawers, some of them locked. My father returned with a bottle of whisky and poured a substantial amount of the golden liquid into the three glasses. The adults stood up and raised their glasses, and I stood up pretending I had a glass in my right hand.

My father said, 'The Leader!' and we responded, 'The Leader!' I put my hand to my mouth and knocked it back.

It was a moment of great meaning and passion. I remember thinking that it must have been just like this when the disciples were together in the locked room, when crowns of fire settled on their heads and they went out and spoke in tongues to people who were amazed. But Jesus was dead and Mosley was still alive. There he was on the mantelpiece, looking at me, rather thin-lipped, I thought, but with piercing eyes and a large right fist which looked as if he had just thumped on the kitchen table and made the fish cakes bounce. It was signed 'O. Mosley' and was my mother's most precious possession. I watched her dust it at least three times a day.

Sometimes I would stand next to the mirror and try to imitate the Mosley look, even place my small fists in front of my chest and try to look aggressive, determined, a man you wouldn't play around with too quickly.

'The Leader!'

I looked up at Jeffrey whose glass was being refilled and then at my mother whose eyes were shining and whose voice sounded like music. The three were laughing and clinking glasses. There was a knock on the door and Lily Hamm came into the warm room looking pale and nervous, but after a while she too was laughing and drinking my father's whisky.

They came up the following evening with the dummy of a new newspaper which would be published and sold in London, a paper called *Union*, which would be edited by one of Mosley's most important followers, a man called Raven Thomson who had written a book about Superman. The newspaper and the movement would be called 'Union' because Mosley's new policy was the unification of Europe, which would end centuries of division between the English and the French, the French and the Germans. Once united, the Europeans would pool their resources so there would be one vast

European Empire, which would be bigger than the British and Roman Empires put together.

'The Leader.'

I could not remember a time in my life when I had not known his name, seen his picture or loved his heroism.

To the right of the mantelpiece from which Sir Oswald glared out at the world there were three seagulls; my mother once told me that when the great man Rudolf Hess flew to Scotland from Germany to try to stop the war, three seagulls flew alongside his plane. Next to the birds on a table was a picture of the Mosley family at their home in Ireland: Sir Oswald, his wife Diana, Max and Alexander. Mosley was wearing a corduroy jacket and looked fit, even a little fat. Max was very thin but had obviously recovered well after being pulled from his mother's breast by the man from Special Branch. I was certain that if we met, Max would be my best friend.

Before I went to bed that night I asked my mother, 'Why is Mr Hamm like St Paul?'

She kissed the side of my face and I breathed in the smell of lipstick and her favourite face powder, which was called Cream Puff Tempting Touch. 'Because when Jesus died the disciples gave up and Peter denied him three times. It took Paul to get them all going again and that's what Mr Hamm is doing, getting them going again.'

'But if Mr Hamm is St Paul, who was Jesus?'

My mother replied: 'Mosley.' Then she told me something which frightened me and which I would never forget. 'You're not to tell people what we talk about in this house. It's all secret. People outside the Mosley movement would never ever understand. Just think that you and Lovene live in two worlds, this one and the world outside 40 Blandford Square.'

I discovered that living in two separate worlds when you are eight years old is not always easy.

The day after my mother's bedtime instructions, the history lesson at school was about great battles and great men in history. We had been told to ask our parents for their opinions. Mr Walker and Mr

Simon sat in on the class.

Most of the children said that the greatest man of all time was Winston Churchill. Mr Walker smiled; Mr Simon looked grim, but applauded loudly when a boy called Hardy stood up and said that the greatest man in the world was Stalin.

Most of the children said the greatest battle of all time was the Battle of Britain or the Normandy invasion.

At the end of the discussion, Mr Walker stood up in his tan tweed suit and said that he thought the greatest battle of all time was Agincourt and that one day we would read about it in William Shakespeare's play *Henry V*. It was great, he told us, because it showed English people could easily beat foreigners if they had the will-power.

Mr Simon rose and said, as if he was addressing a rally of factory workers, that the greatest battle of all time was the Battle of Stalingrad, where Hitler's soldiers had been defeated by Russian peasants.

At the end of the lesson I raised my hand and said that I thought the greatest battle in history was fought at Cable Street in October 1936, when Oswald Mosley marched through the Jewish areas of the East End, and where a man called Tommy Moran had knocked out twelve Communists before he was beaten to the floor by Jews.

The three teachers were stunned into silence. None of the children knew what I was talking about but I remember going beetroot red because I had betrayed my mother's instructions never, whatever the circumstances, to reveal what was spoken about at 40 Blandford Square.

Miss Hill blew a referee's whistle and the school was dismissed. As I left the classroom, Mr Simon said, 'Grundy, come here, will you? Who told you . . . ' then he stopped. I stood looking at him in silence, feeling the red in my face. Then he waved his hand and I was dismissed.

We went to the playground and put on our coloured team bands for a game of football which included the girls. In our team, the blues, was a very pretty dark girl who stayed outside with the wet overcoats during morning prayers. Her name was Vilma and she looked a little like Lovene. She knew Maureen was my girlfriend; Maureen hated Vilma and said she was trying to make me her boyfriend.

A couple of days later Vilma came up to me and said, 'My father told me that the greatest man the world has ever seen was Moses and that the greatest battle ever fought was when the Jews fought the Romans at Masada.'

I thought: 'This is how my mother talks.'

'The Romans surrounded the Jews but they refused to give in so they killed all the women and children and then the men killed themselves. My father told me that even though the Jews were beaten they weren't really because they kept their honour and dignity.'

When I told my mother what Vilma had said she didn't look up from the frying pan. She was cooking sausages for supper. She said that with a name like Vilma the girl must be Jewish and that Jewish parents made their children say things like that, even when they weren't true. Then she did look up and said quite fiercely, which was strange because she hardly ever told me off, 'I told you never to repeat a thing you heard in this house about The Leader.'

It had been snowing, so I put on galoshes over my normal school shoes but my feet were still freezing.

'I'm cold, Beamie.' It was my private name for Lovene.

'You're so weedy,' she said, buttoning up her school mackintosh which was about three sizes too small for her. 'When Mummy had you she said I'd be getting a big brother. I don't know why she told me that. Look what I got,' and she towered over me.

My mother was dressed in a fur coat which my father had bought her when the tenants had paid the final quarter of their annual rent a few days before Christmas. He was in a long dark blue woollen coat. Both wore flash-and-circle badges on their coat lapels. My father's was a simple silver badge symbolising the 'flash of action in the circle of unity', or 'a flash in the pan' as the Communists called it. My mother wore a far more flamboyant design which incorporated the Roman fasces, the symbol of unity and power in the ancient world, on

28

a Union Jack with the letters BUF on it, British Union of Fascists.

The four of us walked to Baker Street Underground Station where an elderly man who owned the shop where my mother bought her expensive face powder lifted his hat and said, 'Good evening, Mrs Grundy.'

A few paces down the road my father muttered, 'Jewboy.'

First we went to Oxford Circus where we climbed up the escalators, which were not working because of the weather, and caught a bus to Trafalgar Square. For a few minutes we stood waiting in the cold outside the National Gallery until a small van stopped and the driver said, 'In you get. Evening, Mrs Grundy. These two your nippers, are they then, Sid?'

We drove past St Martin-in-the-Fields and the enormous column with Nelson on the top looking towards Parliament. I thought: 'Mosley will one day be in charge of Parliament, though he might decide to burn it down like Hitler.'

We were driven to a derelict part of the East End where I overheard the driver talking to my father: 'This was some of the worst damage, Sid. The whole area around dockland was a write-off, but at least it's forcing this bloody government to do something about housing.' He was providing a guided tour and I heard him say, 'That's where the Old Man spoke in '36' and 'Ridley Road, Sid, Ridley Road on the left'. He turned to us in the back seat and said, 'Great days, you two. Great days, coming again. Not long to wait. Great days.'

When he dropped us off, he told my father to catch another bus. Cars went past and I felt a wave of icy water hit my legs. Lovene glared at me so I said nothing.

My mother bent down to me and said, 'In a few minutes you'll see The Leader.'

Then a black van stopped in the road about ten yards from us. 'Sid!' someone shouted. We got in but this time there were a dozen or so people in the back and some were drinking from Watney's brown ale bottles and smoking cigarettes. We all got out when we reached a grey stone school building and walked across the playground where some fresh snow had fallen on top of the black slush. My father stopped several times to greet people he knew as we moved into the main school hall.

Suddenly there were hundreds of people, most of them laughing, slapping one another on the back, and talking very loudly about 'Commies', 'Yids', 'the good old days' and the great days to come now that the Old Man, The Leader, was back.

I noticed that while my father threw himself into the thick of things my mother stood to one side with Lovene and me, politely saying 'Good evening' to East-Enders who wanted to take a closer look at her badge.

One old man knelt down and breathed straight into my face. 'Gonna do a bit of Jew bashin' when you're older?' he leered.

There were Union Jacks and several flags with flash and circles on them set against a blood-red background. My father said, 'It's unbelievable, Edna. At least a thousand people. Two thousand.'

Beside the stage were men with cameras and flashbulbs and every now and again, as one of them took a picture, silence would descend on the room, then the noise, shouting and a lot of laughter, would swell up again. Someone cried out:

> Two, four, six, eight
> Who do we appreciate?

And then the thunderous answer:

> M-o-s-l-e-y
> MOSLEY!

A small man with dancing brown eyes and a Hitler moustache called Alf Flockhart grabbed my father by the arm. He went to the front of the hall and started chanting:

> The Reds, the Reds
> We gotta get rid of the Reds.

And then from the other side of the room, which was like a much larger version of St Paul's school hall, a group of men and women responded:

> *The Yids, the Yids*
> *We gotta get rid of the Yids.*

Someone put on a scratched 78 rpm record. It was a song about Mosley and how he was the leader of millions of people in Britain. Very few people seemed to know the words but I had heard the record played at Blandford Square.

The reporters, still in their hats and coats, took notes. Suddenly the room was filled with the sound of a hymn which instantly froze the audience. Cameras clicked and the room turned white under the flashbulbs. After a few bars of music, I tugged my mother's sleeve, 'The Horst Wessel song, Mummy! Daddy's favourite.' She had her eyes closed. Next to her a woman was crying and several of the men around us raised their right arms. I had never seen my father look so stern. He made his left hand into a fist and placed it over the centre of his chest, his English lips moving to this German song.

> *Comrades, the voices of the dead battalions*
> *Of those who fell*
> *That Britain might be great*
> *Join in our song for they*
> *Still march in spirit with us*
> *And urge us on*
> *To join the Fascist state.*

When the word Fascist was sung the room again went white with flashing bulbs.

> *They're of our blood*
> *and spirit of our spirit*
> *Flushed with the fight*
> *We proudly hail the dawn*
> *See over all the streets*
> *The flash and circle waving*
> *Triumphant standard*
> *Of a race reborn.*

31

At the end of it, Lovene said to me, 'I've got to be at school in the morning and at this rate Mosley won't be here until midnight.'

'But, Beamie,' I replied, 'Mummy says this is the greatest night in the whole of history.'

Close by, I heard a man with a camera say, 'Yes, I agree, but Mosley wasn't a real Fascist, not a Fascist like Mussolini or Hitler. I'd say he was a quasi-Fascist. I mean, it was the time, wasn't it? Intelligent people were either Communists or Fascists, with not much in between. Now it's different. I take your point there. It's different now.'

A man in a trilby hat had a cigarette dangling from his lips but it didn't stop him talking quickly and aggressively. 'It's the same old Mosley, believe you me. Still the same old Mosley, the Jew-baiter. You won't change that one. He's probably worse. They should never have let him out. He'd still be inside if he wasn't a friend of your mate Winston Churchill. I tell you, I went to a lot of this man's meetings before the war and you've never seen anything like it. Anyone who asked a question got thumped, got set upon. Mosley not anti-Jewish? You must be bloody joking!'

A brilliant flash of white light came again but this time it was accompanied by a thunderous roar which must have been heard all over the East End. Mosley entered the room through a side door and walked towards where we were standing, smiling and half saluting at the same time. As he passed, my mother reached out and touched him. He moved quickly forward towards the microphone which was set on a wooden stage more used to morning services and nativity plays. Mosley was smiling, nodding and raising his arm; smiling and holding his head high; and then almost bowing to his followers who were chanting, screaming and yelling their souls out of their bodies as he smiled and lifted his head in acknowledgement once more.

'I touched him. Now I've got the strength to carry on,' my mother said. 'The last time I heard The Leader was at Earl's Court in July 1939. It was the biggest rally for peace the world has ever seen and you were conceived that night.'

Mosley spoke to a hushed audience. Sometimes there was a flash but no one took any notice. The photographers pressed forward to the front of the hall to be closer to Mosley, who looked down and signalled to his supporters to move aside so the journalists could move around more freely. He was a giant of a man, or so it seemed to me, and he pawed the air, a lion in a grey suit. Sometimes he snarled at the microphone. At other times he moved towards it as if he was going to deliver a kiss. Then he would put out his right arm like a boxer, using his left to defend his body.

Whenever he said the words 'international Jewish finance' there was a roar of approval. He repeated the words again, emphasising all the syllables, 'in-ter-na-tion-al Jew-ish fi-nance' and froze at the end of the sentence as the lights flashed and the audience went wild.

Mosley told everyone that night that Britain had been betrayed by the old men of the old parties and it didn't matter whether Labour or the Conservatives were in power because it was the same difference as being run by Tweedledum or Tweedledee. His generation had gone to war against the Germans in 1914 and millions of British lives had been lost. When the survivors returned home, what did they find? The old men of the old parties in soft leather chairs, men who had made a fortune out of a war which had brought Britain to her knees.

Close to the end of the speech, which marked Mosley's return to British politics as the leader of Union Movement, he dropped his voice and became intimate with those listening to him. Later my mother said that he used his voice like an instrument to make wonderful music which brought Mosley and his worshippers together again.

'Every one of us knew that everything for which we thought we'd fought had proved illusion, had proved betrayal. But, my friends, when we rose from the disaster of that experience what happened then? It mattered not. We have not lost, we've gained, we've won. We've won ourselves and that's what matters.'

With those words he lifted the roof off the East End school hall.

I thought: 'We must be like Vilma's Jews who were beaten but who weren't beaten because they kept their dignity and their honour. But if they kept their honour and dignity, why did they have to kill themselves?'

When Mosley left the stage a group of men followed him and I noticed one of them was Jeffrey Hamm, another Alf Flockhart, and another Bill Dodds. When we got outside into the cold and dark, there were hundreds of people milling around smoking, shaking hands and beating their arms round their bodies to keep warm. Motorbike riders returned after escorting Mosley half-way to his house in Chelsea and later rode off again into the night.

We returned to Blandford Square by another circuitous route. My father said that after a meeting like that you couldn't be too careful because the Jews would be out in force and they had formed a vicious razor gang called the '43 Group. We had to watch out for them all the time.

We drank tea before we went to bed. Lovene was exhausted and said she wished she hadn't gone. She had a headache. She told my mother that she had never seen Mosley before in the flesh and did not really want to again. 'He looks like a fox,' she said. My mother said she couldn't believe her ears, her own daughter saying something so appalling about The Leader on the night he returned to Britain.

'A crafty fox,' Lovene added.

'He only mentioned the Jews a couple of times, Edna,' said my father. 'Do you think he's gone soft. I mean, he virtually condemned Fascism and said we'd gone beyond it. Beyond Fascism, beyond democracy. I'd say beyond comprehension. But he still knows how to work you up, doesn't he? But I'm beginning to wonder if this is the same OM, or whether he went soft in prison.'

I climbed onto my father's knee to kiss him goodnight, something I rarely did, but this was a special occasion. I told him that if he thought Mosley had changed and wasn't still anti-Jewish he must be 'bloody joking' and my parents laughed.

In the playground the following day I called Vilma Cohen a Jewish bitch. She ran away and Mr Simon found her crying in the cloakroom.

The next day I was placed in front of the school and caned by Mr Walker, three strokes on the right hand, three on the left. For the next week I was kept inside at lunchtime and made to write lines. Vilma was swiftly taken away from St Paul's primary school and sent to a school for Jewish children in Golders Green, so I couldn't have said 'sorry' even if I'd wanted to.

A week later I told my parents what had happened and tears stung my cheeks as I spoke.

My father stared at me and there was a long silence. Then he looked at my mother and said, 'We've got a right little Jew-baiter here, haven't we, Edna?'

2

Mosley's return to British politics ended our plan to go and live in South Africa.

Maureen said she'd found it on the atlas and it wasn't much to boast about anyway, because although South Africa was pink and belonged to Britain, it wasn't anything like as big as Australia, Canada or India, and seemed to be mostly desert.

We asked Mr Simon how long the Empire would last. He examined us with sharp blue eyes, which looked like two of the marbles we rolled in the gutter after school, and said that all the pink places of the earth should be run by black or brown people. The only black man I had heard of was Paul Robeson, the man who sang 'Ol' Man River' on the radio. Whenever he came on, my father twisted the plastic knob sharply to the left and the deep voice disappeared.

'Communists on the BBC,' he said with disgust in his voice. 'Bloody British Communists.'

May 24 was Empire Day, as well as Queen Victoria's birthday, and the school was given the day off, but not before Mr Walker had addressed us the previous afternoon. He told us that the Empire was one great big happy family of nations and races who shared a common purpose, which was to serve the King, the Queen, Princess Elizabeth, Princess Margaret and the whole Royal Family, the British Government and the Church of England.

He said that when we reached the age of eleven all the boys should join the Boy Scouts, which had been founded by a very great English gentleman and soldier called Baden-Powell, who had fought tyranny during the Boer War in South Africa.

The girls should join the Girl Guides so they could be nurses if ever there was another war, which, 'please God, there will not be in our lifetimes'.

After the Scouts? We boys should join one of the junior military corps. He recommended the Air Training Corps, the ATC, because one of the greatest men who ever lived, a man called T.E. Lawrence, had given up a high Army position after the First World War to become a humble private in the Air Force, which he saw as the first line in Britain's defences. Hadn't he been proved right at the Battle of Britain? Mr Walker looked to the ceiling and I looked as well, hoping to see Mr Lawrence shooting down a plane with a red hammer and sickle on its side.

To make it simple, the headmaster explained that the Empire was exactly like our own families, which had a father, mother, children and religion. In Great Britain the leaders were the English and their children were the Scots, Irish and Welsh. Members of a family could quarrel but before the sun went down they would shake hands like men of honour and courage. Mr Walker said that if ever the Scots broke away from the English, or the Welsh went their own way, then God would be a very disappointed gentleman.

At the end of the Empire Day speech Mr Simon was very bad-tempered. He took off his wire-rimmed spectacles, wiped his forehead with his handkerchief and then coughed into it. Maureen and I watched with amusement as he banged the interlocking doors before storming out of school a few minutes before the bell.

I wondered whether Mr Walker was a secret Mosley supporter because, even though he had caned me, my father had spoken the same way about the British Empire. I'd heard him say to my mother that Mosley was mad if he thought the British people would ever get enthusiastic about the new policy of 'Europe a Nation – Africa the Empire'.

'The silly buggers are giving away India, and next it will be Africa, but there's still Australia, New Zealand and Canada. Who's going to be interested in a union with the French or the Spanish? Germany, yes, but not with the Greeks or the Portuguese. My God, what a thought!'

There was lots of talk about the Empire at our house at the weekends. About a dozen Old Members – people who had been with Mosley before the war – would come to 40 Blandford Square, bringing large bottles of brown ale from the off-licence in Lisson Grove.

I sat close to my mother's feet on a woollen rug which my father had made. It had a large red sailing ship floating on a green sea. All around the ship was blue sky. My father said he'd teach me how to make a carpet one day, but he never did. Lovene would usually sit on the piano stool, somehow untouched by the words and the beery drama of it all.

Lovene and her friend Yvonne – who lived at the end of Blandford Square and who my mother said looked a bit of a tart, 'a blowsy girl' – were in love with a Wembley motorcycle speedway star called Split Waterman. They spent hours looking at his photograph. When they found out from the Wembley Speedway Supporters' Club where Split lived, they began bicycling on Sundays to his house, which was half-way across London, somewhere near Wimbledon, in the hope of catching a glimpse of the daredevil dirt track star. Split had a small moustache like Mosley and Lovene grew angry when I pointed that out. 'He doesn't look at all like Mosley!' she exclaimed. I cannot remember her ever using the words 'The Leader'.

Split had a friend named Bruce Abernathy, also a motorbike racer at Wembley, and once the men waved at the two teenage girls, a wave, said Yvonne, who was blonde with breasts, that changed her life for ever.

'Lovene's thinking about Split or Bruce,' I thought, as the conversation and the beer flowed in the front room of 40 Blandford Square.

When Mr Hamm spoke he used his hands a lot and sometimes flashed his eyes like a lighthouse. Throwing his hands forward to express defiance and resignation, he said, 'The price of beating Hitler was to lose the greatest Empire the world has ever seen and only those who think it was worth destroying the Germans and letting the Russians take half of Europe will smile in days to come.' Mr Hamm told the group of men, most of them East-Enders, that Mosley was going to live in France because he was now a European and had to travel the world to keep up with new ideas and new trends.

Other people kept quiet when he spoke, but when it was over all had something to say about the state of Britain, the Empire and the Jews. Then my mother and sister brought in some sandwiches.

The highlight of the weekend gathering was the arrival of a Fascist called Tommy Moran, the hero of the Battle of Cable Street in 1936. Before the war he had been a heavyweight boxer in the Royal Navy but he had joined Mosley and was the man who had knocked out a dozen Communists in Cable Street when Mosley had marched his men through the Jewish quarter of the East End. My father told me that the cowardly Jews and Communists had all run away and Mosley had been triumphant, so triumphant that the police had walked all the way back to his house in Chelsea with him and his Blackshirts. Tommy Moran was the most popular man in Union Movement after Mosley, my father said.

During the reliving of the massive victory over the Communists at Cable Street, I'd climb onto a chair and place a record on the wind-up gramophone. We had two very precious records, one from Germany of a band playing the Horst Wessel song on one side and an Italian marching song called 'Giovenezza' on the other. Horst Wessel was the Nazi hero who was beaten to death by the Communists.

My favourite was the second record, which had a red and blue flash and circle in the middle by the hole, and on it was The Leader speaking. When I put it on, everyone in the room fell silent and stood up. The voice was deep and full of passion: *'Brother Blackshirts, my comrades in the struggle.'* I would spin my head round as fast as I could to keep the flash and circle clear in my sight.

Mosley told us that he had nothing to offer his followers except the joy of being involved in a struggle which would one day ensure that a great people and a great land would live again. At the end of it, the adults would raise their glasses or cheer, and some would salute, though that was no longer allowed in public, said Mr Hamm, because we had gone beyond Fascism.

'If the Old Man says we're not to use the salute then I reckon we'll lose half the membership, perhaps more,' said Victor Burgess, who was a Union Movement hero because he dared attack Jews in front of a largely Jewish audience on Friday nights at Whitestone Pond on Hampstead Heath. We went there most weeks. Mr Burgess had been razored by the '43 Group of militant Jewish anti-Fascists. He was olive-skinned and there was a rumour that he was the son of a gypsy. He looked like Dr Goebbels, whose picture I had seen in a book that had pride of place on my father's bookshelf. The large red leather-bound volume was entitled *Adolf Hitler* and was published by a German cigarette company in Hamburg. My father told me that after his signed copy of Mosley's book, *The Alternative*, it was his most precious possession. If I was a good Fascist I would one day own both.

I was certainly a good Fascist eight-year-old because whenever fighting broke out at Whitestone Pond I pictured myself as a lone drummer in the Hitler Youth League, ever faithful, ever true against the Red advance and the forces of Jewish reaction. I had seen such a boy in the Hitler book. He had thick blond hair and wore a dark shirt, shorts and long socks. On the front of his circular drum was a flash, just like the one on the Mosley record. When the fighting started I'd stiffen my body and hit an imaginary drum with imaginary drumsticks. *Rat-a-tat-tat*, it went in my head, *rat-a-tat-tat*.

A man shouted '…bloody Fascist bastards' and there'd be a lot of yelling, shoving and pushing, and one of ours would shout back '…bastard Yids'. Then the police would appear and men would be carted off to a van or held down wriggling like landed fish. My mother didn't think I was old enough to become the Horst Wessel of Union Movement and dragged me away to the other side of the road.

'Grab his hand, Lovene, grab his hand! Trevor will get hurt. I've told you once and I won't tell you again. Grab his hand!'

Later, the men would reassemble and we'd go to a friendly

'Movement pub', round the corner in Highgate. The adults would drink beer, while Lovene and I had lemonade and Smith's crisps.

It was like a picnic or an outing to the countryside, and Union Movement people smiled and joked and sometimes raised their arms, tightened their fists, then unclenched them and waved them in the air, imitating their fights with the Jews and Communists. Then they'd laugh and buy each other more beer and the whole thing would start again, because this was an amazing game for adults. It was also a secret game which I couldn't talk about when I went to school because even though it hadn't taken place inside 40 Blandford Square it was definitely connected and therefore forbidden.

At home, after we'd listened to the Mosley record and all the Old Members had left I would go into Lovene's room, next to where my parents slept.

'Brother sister,' I said in as deep a voice as I could, 'my comrade in the struggle.'

We giggled and I forgot for a moment that I was supposed to be a heroic drummer boy and I think Lovene even forgot that she was supposed to be in love with Split Waterman. Or was it Bruce Abernathy?

Lovene failed her eleven plus and went to a school in West Hampstead, a secondary modern, so it was almost certain she would leave school without O levels and get a job somewhere in an office. But she was also a talented violinist and won a scholarship to the Guildhall when she was only twelve. She played beautiful music by the great German composers, Beethoven, Schubert and Schumann. Her painting teacher said she should apply to art school because she could draw extremely well. But when she came home and said she could sit an exam at fifteen to get into Central St Martin's School of Art, my father said, 'Art school? Full of Communists! You won't be going there, my girl. The slump is coming and the best job for you is in the civil service, if they'll have you.'

At eight and a half my future also seemed certain. My mother said that with my interest in the Bible I could become a vicar. She said that because I could sing well, I was bound to be an excellent speaker and would be able to turn the fuddy-duddies of the church into Mosley activists.

'You'll be the Mosley of the Anglican Church,' she told me with absolute certainty in her voice. 'Under slightly different circumstances, your father would have been a vicar. By now he might have been on his way to becoming a bishop. Instead, he married me.' Then she added, in a rare reference to the grandparents we had never seen, 'His mother never forgave me for that and never will. And you must never forget, Trevor, that you're a Maurice, not a Grundy. The Grundys are mean, narrow-minded hypocrites with just one thought in their heads: *Do we look good in public?* But, your father, he's so good, he's so holy. He should have been the vicar of Seaton Sluice. Your father's not meant for this world, he's too good.'

So towards the end of 1948, as I was approaching nine and Lovene moving towards fourteen, my mother took us in search of a vicar to help me get launched onto an unsuspecting Church of England.

We'd arranged to meet the church warden at the side entrance of Christ Church in Bell Street. At the front of the dilapidated grey church was a high bell tower and pillars which were partly hidden by a wooden hoarding with Bisto gravy and Players' cigarettes advertisements on it. The warden, Mr Morrison, was a pale, sickly-looking man in his mid-fifties, with a small hump on his back. He wore glasses which were as thick as the bottom of a bottle of brown ale. He told my mother that he hadn't been in the war for health reasons. I whispered as we were given a conducted tour around the cold, damp, airless building, 'If he wasn't in the war, is he one of us?'

Mr Morrison scrutinised my mother. His mouth was slightly open, his lips were wet and he kept looking at her fur coat. You could see he wanted to touch or stroke it.

'You said you've tried other churches. What made you choose this one? St Peter's is nearer, just round the corner from Blandford Square.'

My mother said she wanted us to attend a High Anglican Church. I looked up at the ceiling which was black with soot. 'I was brought up a Methodist in the north of England but my husband's family was High Church and we want High Church for the children.'

We had tried other churches.

The Sunday before, the three of us sat at the back of St Peter's. My mother insisted on seating us there in case the vicar insulted Hitler in his sermon. He did. He said that we lived in an age when Evil had revealed its true face and it was the face of the madman Adolf Hitler who had killed six million Jews. The vicar said that no one had known the true scale of Hitler's crimes until now and that is why the Nazis had been put on trial and executed. I knew what was coming and so did Lovene. We closed our prayer and hymn books, adjusted our galoshes and stood up even before my mother. We all made a point of bowing to the Cross before walking out into the cold.

The man who had handed out the hymn books ran after us. 'Are you all right? Is anyone sick? Can I help?'

My mother turned sharply to him. 'You can tell that vicar of yours that yes, we are sick, sick and tired of hearing about the Germans. Ask him about Bomber Harris and Dresden.'

The man stopped as if someone had shot him.

On the way home I thought, but why has she broken the rules and shown who we are outside 40 Blandford Square?

For the rest of the day my mother was terribly angry and ordered Lovene to turn off Vera Lynn who was singing her famous song about the White Cliffs of Dover. 'There should be a special church for people like us,' she announced to the kitchen walls. When *Family Favourites* came on the radio she cheered up a bit and said we'd try Christ Church next time.

My mother said, 'I'm sure Christ Church is what we're looking for. Quite sure.'

We continued our guided tour. Mr Morrison switched on a very weak light which partly illuminated a fresco above the high altar of the church. It showed the Risen Lord on a cloud blessing the world. Floating next to Him and smiling were golden angels. Below them was a small group of disciples who, I knew from my mother, had betrayed their leader. They were now waiting for courage, for baskets of fire to settle on their heads so they might speak again, but in a way that would set the world alight. They were waiting for something to make them live again and there He was, looking down, and there they were looking up. Mr Morrison told us the fresco had been painted by a man called Thomas Cave who was born in Marylebone in 1820. 'That was five years after the overthrow of Napoleon. He was a terrible man, like Hitler, but the English got rid of him and made him live on an island. Did you know that, Trevor? Do they teach you about Napoleon at school?'

I felt my mother stiffen and got ready for the walkout, but it did not come.

At the end of our short tour Mr Morrison said, looking curiously at my heavily made-up mother, 'Well, Mrs Grundy, we're glad to welcome you and your family and hope that after the service on Sunday you'll come and have breakfast with us at Church House down the road. Bring some bread or rolls. We do the tea. Then I'll introduce you to the rector, Father Spencer.' He also mentioned that he was Akela of the Thirteenth St Marylebone Cub Pack and that I might like to join.

For the first few weeks none of us went to Church House for breakfast. We kept to ourselves in the back pew of the church just in case, but after our second visit a boy of my own age asked me if my dad had been killed in the war. I told him no, that he worked on Sundays.

'So what did he do during the war?' asked Ginger Griffiths.

I repeated what I had been told to say so many times before. 'Special duties. He was on very important, very special duties.'

After a month I was invited to join the choir. The organist and choirmaster, Mr Barratt, wore a wig, which he used to hold in place when he got excited. He would sweat and pant and his eyes would come out on stalks when he tried to make a special point about music. He told me, 'You could get a scholarship to St Paul's Choir School but your voice needs training. Do you want me to train your voice?'

One Friday night while I was changing from my choir cassock back into my shorts and blazer my mother came to collect me and I heard her say to Mr Barratt, 'Be careful with Trevor because he's got a weak chest. You can see how pale and nervous he is when I'm not around.'

I walked home with her, choking back my tears because I was certain Ginger had overheard what she had said. Before we reached the door I said, 'Why do you always tell everyone I'm weak? Ginger thinks I'm a girl. He told the others that I'm a Mummy's boy. *And* my bike hasn't got a crossbar. You're always saying I'm like Uncle Rolly but I'm not. I'm Trevor and I'm all right even though I cough a lot.'

The following week after choir practice Mr Barratt took me to one side. 'Let's have a look at you. I think you look fine and let me tell you this, young man, you have a really wonderful voice. I don't think I've ever heard such a clear, almost crystal clear, voice in a long time.'

On Sunday I waited for Mr Barratt's organ cue as the congregation moved from their pews to the altar rail for communion. My high soprano voice resounded and echoed throughout the almost empty nineteenth-century building.

> *O lamb of God,*
> *That taketh away the sins of the world*
> *Have mercy upon us.*
>
> *O lamb of God*
> *That taketh away the sins of the world*
> *Grant us Thy peace.*

After she was confirmed by the Archbishop of Canterbury in the crypt of St Paul's Cathedral, Lovene joined my mother at the communion rail. I saw them through my half-open eyes because I was supposed to be praying and my heart swelled with pride as they reached out to receive the Eucharist, right hand over left to take the sacred wafer. Then they would gently take hold of the bottom of the cup which the rector tipped towards them, the golden cup which contained the blood of Christ.

Thomas Cave's fresco was clear in the morning light, even though it needed cleaning and repairing. I stared at the picture, at the face of Christ and turned to see my mother's wonderful profile looking down and then up with utter confidence into the deep brown eyes of the rector.

I went as red as a beetroot when I heard that my mother was waiting to see Mr Morrison. I had told her that three boys who had joined the Christ Church wolf cubs with me had been made seconders while I remained an ordinary cub.

At the end of the Wednesday cubs' meeting after we'd *dib-dib-dibbed* and *dob-dob-dobbed*, promised *Akela, we'll do our best* and said goodnight, the rector took me aside and said that we were going upstairs to his flat.

I sat next to my mother in my green uniform, which had no badges on the sleeves. The three adults spoke about me as if I wasn't there, although two or three times I saw the rector frown at me.

Mr Morrison said that I never mixed with the other boys, that I avoided games, especially games that involved touching other children. He said perhaps the other cubs resented me because I lived in Blandford Square, which they thought was the posh part of Marylebone because they were mainly from council flats in Lisson Grove, Bell Street or Church Street market. He said that I wasn't popular enough to be made a seconder and that he wouldn't be changing his mind.

My mother said then I wouldn't be a cub any more but I would stay on in the choir because I was the best singer and that was probably why I hadn't been made a seconder.

Shortly afterwards she took me to see Dr Norris at his surgery in the Church Street market area. Opposite the surgery were dilapidated shops and bright red blocks of council flats. On Saturdays, the whole area was turned into a vast market, with barrow-boys selling everything from pins to pop records.

Mother asked Dr Norris what she could give me because I had started to stammer and was losing weight. 'He's as pale as a sheet and he'll never pass his eleven plus at this rate.'

The doctor told me to undress and he examined my chest. My mother looked at him intently. 'He's got a weak chest. Always has since he was born.' The doctor put the ice-cold metal head of the stethoscope against my chest and listened, moving it carefully all over the top half of my body. Then he banged the area under my knee and my leg flicked up automatically, which made me laugh.

'There is nothing at all wrong with his chest, Mrs Grundy, and there's nothing physically wrong with your son. He's thin, yes, but lots of children are thin. How old is he?' Dr Norris looked at my national health card. 'Eight and three quarters.'

'And the stammer. Why is he stammering?' my mother demanded.

The doctor sat back in his wooden armchair and explained that it was a nervous condition. A child knew what he wanted to say but felt that if he said it there would be some form of punishment by the parents.

My mother looked angry. 'No one punishes him for anything in our house, although he was caned at school, but only once. I don't think his father has ever smacked him. I certainly haven't.' Then she told Dr Norris about me not becoming a seconder at cubs, again as if I wasn't there.

Dr Norris's partner, an aggressive Scot called Dr MacGuire, who wore steel-rimmed glasses and never smiled, rapped on the door and came in. 'The Irish army's here. Six kids with her this time. Measles.'

For me, the doctor prescribed walks in Regent's Park and cod liver oil.

The following day, before I went off to school, my mother rubbed some of her rouge into my cheeks and said, 'There. Now you look much better.'

When I got to the corner of the square I turned as usual and saw her give me an extra-enthusiastic salute. I heard her say something before she smiled and waved. I smiled and waved back. 'PJ, Mummy,' I said, 'PJ.'

When I was out of sight I rubbed my face as hard as I could with my handkerchief and tied a knot in it to remind myself to wash it in the basin before I got home that afternoon.

The rector of Christ Church, Christopher Spencer, was quite a small man and very dark. He had lots of shiny black hair which made him look taller than he was. His skin was a dark olive colour and he always looked as if he needed a shave. He had deep brown, almost black eyes and a wonderfully warm, welcoming smile. When he laughed he looked very young, like a student dressed up as a vicar. He rolled his own cigarettes and was a chain-smoker who constantly dropped ash on the carpet and down his cassock, which he brushed off or rubbed into the cloth with his nicotine-stained right hand.

My mother said the rector was just how she had always imagined St John, the disciple Jesus loved. Peter was the tough one but at the Last Supper Jesus had put his head on John's breast. She said she liked the fourth gospel best because it told the truth about the Jews. When they had cried for the blood of Jesus, they had condemned themselves for ever, she declaimed like an actress. But why did she always smile?

The rector sat on the only soft chair in the tiny kitchen. We sat round him as if we had invited the hungry prophet in the Bible into the house to eat with us. The room was so small you had to be careful when you moved. It contained a sink, a gas cooker, a mangle, a long wooden cabinet made of pine, a table and four chairs and a large picture of Oswald Mosley in a black fencing jacket over the mantelpiece.

The first time the rector saw it, he asked who it was. A sporting hero much admired by Mr and Mrs Grundy?

My mother looked him full in the face, her eyes flashing on and off like beacons, a characteristic which was common among people who had met and loved Sir Oswald Mosley.

'That's Sir Oswald Mosley, the greatest living Englishman.'

He cut short his first visit after meeting Mosley-of-the-wall but came back the following week and then the week after, and for a long time 40 Blandford Square was his second home.

Once, after the rector had sat with me for over an hour in a vain attempt to make me understand the basics of arithmetic, my mother said, 'He's more like your father than your real father.' And added after a long pause, 'Pity he isn't.'

My father knew when the rector had been round to our house.

'Damned vicar with his cigarette smoke,' he said after returning from Hampton Court, red in the face, tired and on occasion smelling strongly of beer.

Sometimes in the summer he wouldn't finish work until seven or eight o'clock at night, then he would go and have a few pints at the Mitre, which was then owned by the great Welsh heavyweight boxer, Tommy Farr, famous for having fought the even greater Joe Louis.

'Had a few pints with Tommy Farr,' he would say when he got home. He banged the door and an atmosphere of violence entered.

Towards the end of 1948 his drinking got worse, rows between him and my mother grew fiercer and sometimes we saw them push one another around. Lovene and I dreaded Sunday at ten o'clock when the front door opened and his heavy, sometimes stumbling footsteps were heard coming along the corridor.

But when my father was still at work, which was most of the time, and the rector was at the house, the subject would inevitably end up with Mosley. It was like a game of tennis between my mother and the rector, with Lovene and I the onlookers, our heads moving from right to left, from left to right, to see and hear who was going to win the decisive point of the match.

'He might be a clever man as you say, Mrs Grundy, but why was he so anti-Jewish? How can you be a Christian and, at the same time, be anti-Jewish? Our Lord was Jewish.'

'And look what happened to him!' she snapped back at the man of God. 'Who killed him? The Romans hammered in the nails but who told them to?'

And then: 'Mosley doesn't hate all Jews. He always says, we don't hate them for what they are, only for what they do. He means the financiers who put money before Britain, the people who dragged us into the war against Germany because they had their money tied up in Poland. The Jews are behind all revolutions, Rector. Did you know that about ninety per cent of the first Communist government under Lenin was made up of Jews? The Spanish Civil War was organised by Jews who encouraged the working class to rape nuns. We've got pictures. Do you want to see what they did to nuns in Spain, Rector, or will that put you off your supper?'

The rector lit another cigarette and wiped the ash from his cassock with his long brown fingers. 'Mrs Grundy, I find you a puzzling woman. You're the only person at Christ Church who has cripples from the hostel round for supper and yet you hate the Jews. All those pictures, they're propaganda. I know where you get those books. From Spain. I could show you pictures far worse if I went along to the *Daily Worker* and asked for them but they'd be Fascist atrocities, not Communist atrocities.'

'So what would you do if the Commies went into Christ Church and started raping the youth club girls?'

'I'd do what the founders of the church did, Mrs Grundy, I'd be a martyr.'

'A *tomata*,' she said. And they'd laugh.

Then she would look at the clock and if it was close to ten o'clock on a Sunday night the rector would say thank you for supper, brush down his cassock one more time and leave. Lovene and I would listen for our father's footsteps and a few seconds later witness the menacing and animal-like sniffing of the kitchen air and later, from our respective beds, hear the increasingly frightening end-of-weekend row in which strange words were used which I didn't understand, words expressed with a hammer-like violence that so often sent me scurrying into Lovene's bed, where I would curl up in a tiny, frightened ball. Then they would go to bed and their voices would be normal. Later we could hear their bedsprings and my father almost shouting again: 'There you are, there you are. Was that better than that bloody old man Lawes?'

We would squeeze and cuddle each other hard and later I would creep back into my own bed and wake there in the morning, when, miraculously, everything would be normal again.

One evening, when my father had finished the Hampton Court season, the rector, his curate Father Cooper, who for some reason was always called Mr Cooper, and Jeffrey Hamm and his wife all came to supper. At my mother's insistence, Mr Hamm was to give the two clerics the official interpretation of Mosley's career, which both men had requested to hear.

'Look at Sir Oswald's track record,' Jeffrey Hamm said softly, with his slight Welsh accent. 'Mosley nearly lost his leg fighting for Britain during the First World War and then he served with the Royal Flying Corps in the days when the machines were held together with bits of glue and rubber bands.' We all laughed. 'He was the youngest MP since Pitt and when he was in his early thirties he was one of the ministers in the Labour government made responsible for solving the unemployment problem. There were three million people unemployed and people like Mr and Mrs Grundy saw for themselves what it had done to community life in Northumberland, where most of the mines came to a halt because cheap coal was being imported from Poland. Can you imagine? From Poland! It was only after he'd tried everything possible to get the government to adopt the policy of Keynes that Mosley resigned. That was after he'd addressed the House of Commons following the publication of the Mosley Memorandum, which even his enemies say is the greatest speech ever made there. Mosley said that unemployment could be cured if the government embarked on great road-building programmes, if it put men to work knocking down slums and building decent homes for the people lauded as 'heroes' after the First World War. All the great historians today say that Mosley was the best thinker in the House and that's why his imaginative plans were rejected – they were just too far ahead of the time. But only when his constructive plans were ignored by the old men of the old parties did Mosley resign, form the New Party and finally the British Union of Fascists. He went to Italy and Germany and saw what Mussolini and Hitler were doing for their people – building roads, clearing slums and marshes, making people stand up straight with pride in their faces. Yes, I admit there was violence but it was violence inspired by Communists and Jews who were in an unhappy alliance to stop progress in Britain unless it was the sort of progress they approved of, progress authorised and rubber-stamped by their paymasters in the Kremlin.'

I thought my mother would applaud, or salute. I wanted to touch Mr Hamm to get some strength for my schoolwork, particularly arithmetic, just as my mother had gained strength from Mosley when

Union Movement was founded.

'Leave Mr Hamm alone,' said my mother, but I managed to touch his sleeve.

'This was the man the gutter press called a traitor in the war. But he never had a trial. He was never charged. Mr Grundy was never charged. I wasn't and at least eight hundred of us were never charged. So much for British justice. They'd have let Mosley die in prison if it hadn't been for Winston Churchill, who knew Mosley and knew he wasn't a traitor, but we'll have to wait thirty years before the cabinet papers are released to see who was telling the truth. Thirty years, that's until 1978, until the government of the day dares release the papers which deal with Norman Birkett's cross-examination of The Leader – Mosley – in 1940. What a disgrace!'

'Well, I'm sure Mosley will be in power long before then and he'll be able to release them himself,' said Mr Cooper, who perhaps thought he was involved in a college debate. He was a large open-faced man of twenty-four, with a bright and breezy manner picked up from his days at a minor public school in southern England.

The rector half laughed but no one else even twitched a face muscle.

'Mr Hamm,' said the rector, who was trying to light yet another hand-rolled cigarette. 'The foreign interests you talk about, which Mrs Grundy talks about, were being killed in their tens of thousands by the people your leader was praising so generously throughout the thirties, when atrocities in Germany were happening. Surely you haven't forgotten *Kristallnacht* in 1938 when the Nazis went on the rampage and smashed up every shop owned by the Jews? It was around that time that your precious leader tried to march thousands of his uniformed followers through the Jewish part of the East End. Of course there was violence but Mosley caused it, not the Jews. It was Mosley, we all know that.'

I waited for a sharp return volley from my mother but she was silent and looking down. Somehow with Mr Hamm and my father in the room it was no longer tennis, or any other game.

'The Jews weren't allowed to practise any of the professions under

Hitler and after he came to power the greatest scientists, philosophers, religious leaders and musicians in the world fled the land of their birth and came here or went to America.' There was a long pause and the rector said to my father, 'Mr Grundy, how would you feel if you'd married a Jewess and then someone had come along to you and said that your children weren't British?'

There was a terrifying silence and I felt as though we were back in the cupboard at Loudoun Road, that the doodlebug was about to fall and that my mother would soon start counting backwards from ten.

My father looked at the rector. His face was red and I noticed his hands. The right one had formed a fist.

The rector coughed and twiddled his Rizla roller. 'Mr Grundy, come now. It was just an example. It was an example of what might have happened, because, you must admit, a great many Germans married non-German women and . . .'

My father pushed aside his cup of tea, stood up, walked along the corridor, opened the front room door and closed it silently, with great control considering the look on his face.

The rector looked at Mr Cooper, who looked at his watch, then at my mother. He smiled and, after inhaling deeply and then blowing out again, said, 'Well then, Mrs Grundy.'

After a few minutes' embarrassed silence we heard music from the gramophone. It was from Wagner's famous opera, *Tannhäuser*. My father had the full score and sometimes he conducted it in front of an imaginary audience. I had seen him through a crack in the door.

I whispered to my mother as the rector and Mr Cooper moved almost silently towards the door which led to the Square, 'If we all go into the front room I'll ask if I can play the Horst Wessel song. Daddy says that when he hears the Germans singing it properly it always makes him feel better.'

During the late summer days of 1948 a letter landed on the mat at 40 Blandford Square which changed our lives.

I took it along the corridor and handed it to my father, who was finishing his breakfast before leaving for Hampton Court. He opened it and I saw his hands start to shake. With a mixture of delight and fear on his face, he handed it to my mother and said, 'It's from Seaton Sluice.' Then, like a child, 'It's from my mother and father.'

My mother looked at the back of the envelope and handed it to him. She was ashen-faced.

I wanted quickly to rush and tell Lovene what I had just seen and heard, but she had already left for school. Neither of us had ever grasped the fact that our parents had parents, although we had heard short, sharp, rude references to them. My mother told me about the mean-spirited Grundys. My father called my mother's mother 'that bitch of a woman'.

I asked my father to read the letter. I remembered Lovene had said to me once during one of our bedtime conversations, 'If we ever met them, what would we say? Hello, Mr and Mrs Grundy, or hello, Grandma and Grandpa?'

I looked at the bottom of the letter and noticed that the handwriting was almost identical to my father's; it sloped forward and was very neat. The letter was signed *Tom Grundy*. My father read it nervously.

Dear S. Grundy,

Excuse me if I am writing to the wrong person but a friend of mine was recently at Hampton Court and he told me that he had had some pictures taken of him and his wife by a street photographer who looked in his late thirties or early forties. When the pictures arrived at his office in Newcastle the stamp on the back said 'S. Grundy, 40 Blandford Square, Marylebone, London NW1'. He mentioned this to me last week when I was in Newcastle.

Perhaps I am writing to the wrong person but we had a son called Sidney Grundy and we have not seen or heard from him since long before the war. He might have been killed but there is a remote chance this letter will reach my son. If this is you, please write to your mother and father.

Perhaps I will receive a reply and I pray it is you, Sidney.

With best wishes

Tom and Elizabeth Grundy
The Hillocks, Marine View, Seaton Sluice, Northumberland.

I had never seen my father cry, but his eyes filled with tears and he left the room hurriedly. A little later I heard the front door close. My mother was staring at the wall as if she'd seen a ghost.

A week after that fateful letter dropped onto the mat Lovene and I were told that we were going to Newcastle on the Flying Scotsman.

Like an excited, mischievous little boy, my father described Whitley Bay to us and its famous White City, where the big dipper would take us to the top of the world. He gave us seven shillings and sixpence each as spending money and promised us more as time went by. We were to be away for five weeks and would be back a week late for school, but that would be explained to headmasters and form masters in letters, so there was no need to worry.

Before we left for King's Cross Station my mother parted my hair, plastered it down with Vaseline and dabbed some rouge onto my face with a powder puff. 'He looks so pale,' she said. Lovene turned away.

As the train pulled out of the station Lovene took me to the lavatory, dampened her handkerchief under the tap and rubbed my face until I thought it would bleed. 'You're nearly nine. Stop being such a weed!'

I said, crying, 'But Beamie, it's not my fault she treats me like a girl.'

I remember the journey from London to Newcastle as one of the most exciting of my life. It was our first trip together away from our parents. More than an hour had passed before I realised I hadn't missed Mummy.

We stepped onto the platform at Newcastle to be met by a small, bright-eyed man with ruddy cheeks, the personification of health and good humour, and his rather large, Scottish wife. Lovene asked the much-rehearsed question: 'Shall we call you Mr and Mrs Grundy or Grandpa and Grandma?'

Elizabeth Grundy's voice was sure but her face registered bewilderment, 'Why Grandma and Grandpa, of course, Lovene.'

We travelled by bus from Newcastle to Whitley Bay and there I glimpsed the White City for the first time with its sparkling dome and the big dipper, high as the sky. We changed to another bus, which took us along the coast road to Seaton Sluice. The bus stopped outside a pub, the Astley Arms, and we retraced our steps for a few yards to a red-brick, two-storeyed house called 'The Hillocks'.

Lovene was given a large room at the top of the house and I had a small one next to hers. I opened the window and a wonderful breeze blew the smell of the sea into my face. My grandparents' house overlooked a wide expanse of grass known as The Links, which led down through the dunes to an enormous sandy bay. To the left in the distance I could see Blyth lighthouse shimmering in the sun.

'That's Whitley Bay,' said Lovene, pointing in the opposite direction. 'That's where Mummy's sister lives.'

Our grandparents wanted to know about our lives in London and why I looked so pale. 'Doesn't he get any fresh air, Lovene?' my concerned grandmother asked. 'Your father says he takes him to the park to play football but it doesn't look much like it.'

After only a couple of days I said to my sister, 'I don't want to go back to London. We could live here.'

On Friday night, while Lovene was playing the violin accompanied by her grandfather on the organ, my grandmother appeared in the bathroom with her sleeves rolled up. 'Now,' she said, 'I don't want to see any more of that muck on your hair. I don't know what yer mam does to you in London but she's not here to do it now.' And she soaped my head until I was dizzy.

Afterwards she showed me some photographs of my father when he was my age. He looked so sad and serious. 'He was going to be a vicar until he met your mother. He had a lovely singing voice and was in the choir, just like you. Your grandpa plays the organ beautifully.'

I said, 'I'm going to be a vicar, otherwise the Jews will take over the Church of England. My mother says she'll live with me in the vicarage but I don't know what will happen to Daddy. Can he live here? He always says he likes the north better than London and loves Seaton Sluice.'

She stared at me strangely, but replied, 'You're talking daft.'

In the mornings we were let loose. We were given sandwiches and told not to return until four o'clock. We bought sweets and soft drinks at the nearby corner shop from a lovely, smiling, blonde lady called Mrs Vera Hall. 'My word,' she would say every morning, 'Londoners have got a sweet tooth.'

I was terrified of the sea but would duck my head into the waves to impress Lovene, who would shout, 'Weed!'

We hired a tent for sixpence and played a game based on the film *Blue Lagoon*. A couple are stranded on an island but they fall in love. I was Donald Houston and Lovene was Jean Simmons but the game soon ended. 'How can you be in *Blue Lagoon* when you can't swim?'

I became tanned and put on weight. My body began to develop and there were muscles in my arms and legs which I had never seen before. My hair blew in the wind and I began to lose the stammer I had acquired after the caning at St Paul's.

'Do you like it here, then, lads and lasses?' my grandfather asked in a singsong voice.

'We love it here, Grandpa,' I sang back. 'We don't want to go home again.'

'But you're gonna have to because you don't belong to us, yer know.'

One day when we'd walked to a small rocky bay to go climbing on a tall pillar of rock called Charlie's Garden, a boy in long trousers appeared and shouted to us, 'Do ya want help?' He was easily identified as a local because of his strong accent and Lovene had been told to be careful about boys from the village. I shouted back, 'I'm okay,' wondering whether he could tell that I was a weed without even knowing me. He came over to talk to us. His name was Eddie Turney and he played football with the local side. He was sixteen and his father was a miner.

That night I heard my grandmother saying, '. . . nice boy he might be, Lovene, but the Turneys are Catholics and that's not good enough because of your grandpa's position. And I'm responsible while you're here and you're not to . . .'

Later I heard Lovene crying, so I went in to cuddle her. 'Go away,' she said, 'how could you understand?'

Towards the end of our first holiday up north we were put onto a bus to go to see our other grandparents, Grandpa and Grandma Maurice, and Auntie Dora. They still lived in Whitley Bay but in a tiny council house.

We ate cake with them and I played with Dora, my mother's older sister, who was the same height as me. My grandmother wore a black dress and had a black veil. My grandfather said very little but showed me how to cut up tobacco and put it in his pipe. I was most impressed with his small silver penknife.

The room was in darkness and most of the furniture was also a dark colour. On one of the small tables there was a large book like a Bible but when I examined it there was no Matthew, Mark, Luke or John. When Auntie Dora saw me, she said we should go outside and play.

When we returned to 'The Hillocks' Grandpa Grundy said, 'Well, who do you like the best, your Grandpa Maurice or your Grandpa Grundy?' And we both cried, 'Our Grandpa Grundy.' He put his arm around Lovene and kissed her cheek.

On the bus back to Newcastle we waved goodbye to Seaton Sluice. When we passed Charlie's Garden Lovene swore me to lifelong secrecy (and if I ever told I'd get the worst Chinese burn on my arm in the history of Chinese torture): Eddie Turney had kissed her up against the rocks and was going to write to her.

We arrived back at King's Cross to be met by my mother, who said my father had come home drunk from Hampton Court the previous night and had called her a slut. She was thinking of leaving him and taking Lovene. We got onto the bus which took us to Baker Street and struggled with the suitcases past Dorset Square and Marylebone Station, along Harewood Avenue and into Blandford Square, which looked big and dirty.

That night I heard my parents fighting, then a long silence and a lot of grunting followed by, 'Was that better than old man Lawes?' I said to Lovene that I wanted to go back to Seaton Sluice.

When I was ready for school the next morning my mother said my hair looked a mess and reached for a tin of Vaseline. Lovene turned on her. 'Leave him alone! For the first time he looks like a real boy and you're going to put more of that disgusting grease on him. Leave him alone!'

That night I overheard my mother tell my father that Lovene must be having a bad period.

I passed on the message from my grandparents that I should get more fresh air and the following Sunday my father said he'd take me for a walk after evensong. When I got back to the house at seven thirty he was waiting for me in the front room. He opened a drawer in the sideboard and put a knuckle-duster into his jacket pocket. I'd seen it before. It had 'Peggy' engraved on it and was kept in the drawer next to a gun in a leather case.

We walked down Edgware Road and past the Metropolitan Music Hall. Just before the Blue Hall cinema there was a shop full of armour and swords where my father always stopped to look in the window. At Marble Arch we waited by the corner where some of my father's friends who came to see us sometimes appeared. When they arrived, we all crossed the road to Speakers' Corner and my father told me to wait by the railings. I stood next to a policeman.

There were dozens of speakers on platforms and after a while it got dark and I heard my father shout, 'Jewboy!' Some fighting broke out and the policeman walked quickly to the crowd of scuffling men. Then my father reappeared, took my hand and we crossed the road and walked back down Edgware Road. We stopped at Church Street and the group re-formed. They were laughing and pretending to hit one another. My father went into a pub with them but returned with a lemonade and a bag of Smith's crisps for me. He laughed and said he'd forgotten to put his teeth back in.

An Irish girl with beautiful eyes but very bad teeth noticed me. 'Out here on your own, are you, darling? When you're a big boy I'll take you home with me.'

The following week my father said at supper, 'Next time Lovene and Trevor go up north I think we should go with them, Edna. There's an awful lot of damage that needs repairing.'

I hadn't noticed any and surely Grandma would have had it fixed. She kept 'The Hillocks' spotless and Grandpa Grundy said she was the most house-proud woman in Seaton Sluice.

3

Mr Simon told the class that only a handful of pupils had passed the eleven plus. In 1951 a three-tier system existed at secondary school level, with the more intellectual children going to grammar schools, the 'semi-intellectual' going to central schools and the less intellectual going to secondary modern schools. Mr Simon read out the names and kept mine until last. I was thunderstruck because I was hopeless at arithmetic.

'One of us got in by the skin of our teeth but got in, nevertheless. We had to have one of the Grundy children get to a grammar school,' he said, smiling at me. 'Even though Lovene should have been the one, not you,' he added and I felt my face burn crimson. 'Your sister was too busy looking after her *little brother Trevor* to learn properly but, anyway, I think she'll succeed in life – an artist or a musician, that's my bet. Anyway, well done, and don't be so embarrassed about it.'

At lunchtime Maureen went home crying. She was going to a secondary central. Most of the class were destined for secondary moderns. After lunch she said, 'My father says that a secondary central school is just as good as a grammar school and *better* in some ways because the children who want their O levels work harder.'

It was the end of our four-year love affair.

My mother was overjoyed when I told her my exam results and immediately made two telephone calls. The first was to the rector at

Christ Church, whose support, she said, was needed to get me into the right kind of Church of England school; the second was to Alf Flockhart, the secretary of Union Movement at 302 Vauxhall Bridge Road, to let everyone there know the Grundy family's good news.

Later she said, 'The rector will use all his influence to get you into the right school and Alf said The Leader is delighted. He telephoned him in Paris.'

I was enrolled at a south London grammar school, despite a bad interview.

When asked to spell the name of the school I wrote 'Tennyson's,' which was extremely unobservant, said the headmaster, a small, spiky man who looked like the drawing of Punch in the famous magazine.

Archbishop Tenison's Grammar School had been founded in 1685 in the crypt of St Martin-in-the-Fields. Now the top floor of the red-brick school building overlooked the famous Oval, home of Surrey cricket club, and we were allowed to play two matches a year against other London schools on that sacred turf.

I was put into the C stream, which meant that unless I could work my way up to the A or B stream by the time I was thirteen I would not learn Latin, so essential for my future career as a vicar.

As soon as my beautiful royal-blue blazer was bought from the school shop in Buckingham Palace Road I went walking with my mother at the 'Jewish' end of Regent's Park. My mother loved parading around that part of the park, looking at the ducks and swans but also watching the Jewish women with their French or Scandinavian au pair girls. She was on nodding terms with several women and pointed out to them the mitre on my school badge. 'Archbishop Tenison's was founded in *1685* by the *Archbishop of Canterbury.*' I went red and prayed she wouldn't also tell them that she was a land*lady.* I had seen faces from Sherborne Place turn away and then snigger when she'd said this in the local shops.

One woman whom we'd seen walking with her poodle into Dorset Mansions said to my mother while I was being displayed, 'Why aren't you sending him to one of *our* schools?'

My mother smiled and we walked on, around the Inner Circle and into Queen Mary's Gardens to admire the fountain.

'What did that lady mean, one of *our* schools?' I asked.

My mother looked delighted. 'Oh, I think some of those silly women think that I'm Jewish. Your grandmother's mother was Spanish and that's why Lovene and I have such dark eyes. Jewish women think they're paying you some sort of compliment when they say that.' She laughed. 'If only they knew!' And we walked on.

'If only they knew, Mummy.' And together we said, 'PJ.'

Then, as always, I was conscious of receiving my mother's full, undivided attention. Shared and secret moments such as this reinforced my belief that, as long as she approved, I could do anything.

That night she hung up my blazer and placed it in the wardrobe next to her fur coat.

'Never let me down, Trevor,' she said without looking at me. 'You're never to let me down because I've put all my hopes in you . . . you and The Leader.'

Lovene was now sixteen. She had left a secondary central school in Hampstead the year before and had gone to work in the typing pool at the Ministry of Local Government and Housing. She went to night school and started to learn shorthand and German. She played her violin increasingly rarely, mainly because my father was a complete dictator when it came to music.

One evening, with a crowd of Union Movement people in the front room of the house, my father insisted Lovene play for them. She bit her lip and said that she'd been learning a piece by Mendelssohn. My father broke the room's eerie silence.

'Mendelssohn! That Jewboy! We won't be playing any Mendelssohn rubbish in this house!'

A voice said, 'Your father's right you know, Lovene. We don't want to listen to Jewish music. It stinks.'

Lovene left the room and went to her friend Yvonne's basement flat. My father went looking for her and she came home crying. He shouted, 'You're a disgrace.' And she never touched the violin again.

In October 1951, at the start of Mosley's winter campaign, Lovene was asked to present Lady Mosley with a bouquet of flowers at the Movement's annual dinner, held in an upstairs room of a pub in Victoria.

There were about two hundred people in the room when she made the presentation and Lady Mosley, playing royalty, smiled and thanked her. The Leader looked on and beamed and just about everyone in Union Movement under the age of thirty fell in love with Lovene, including a good-looking public schoolboy called John Wood, who was about to do his national service in the Suez Canal Zone of Egypt.

From the moment that I entered Archbishop Tenison's I excelled at religious studies. Although I got only ten or fifteen per cent for arithmetic, I regularly came top in religion, with ninety sometimes ninety-nine per cent, and became the favourite of the religion and music teacher, Mr Burton.

At the end of the first term all the parents were invited to meet the housemasters and teachers and my mother, dressed to the nines, stated in front of Mr Burton that I wanted to be ordained.

The following day, Mr Burton announced this fact to the whole of form 1C, most of whom came from the council flats around the Oval, or from Brixton. I was one of the few boys from north of the River Thames, which already made me odd, without having the added label of clergyman hung round my neck. I had also started playing the violin, which probably increased my alienation from my rough-and-tumble peer group.

My mother told me that the earliest I could be ordained was twenty-three and the question was, should I go straight from Archbishop Tenison's to university, or to theological college? The subject would frequently be discussed by what my father called 'The Holy Trinity', which assembled on a regular basis at 40 Blandford Square when he was working at Hampton Court. The Trinity was made up of the rector, Mr Spencer, the curate, Mr Cooper, and the organist and choirmaster, Mr Barratt.

'University,' suggested Mr Cooper. 'Trevor needs the chips

knocking off his shoulder and university is the place for that.'

'What chips?' asked my mother aggressively.

The rector changed the subject. 'A college is just as good, Mrs Grundy, but Trevor has first to be accepted by a church selection committee. He can't just become a vicar overnight, you know.'

Clifford Barratt was a wonderful pianist. After supper he sat down at my father's piano, a Chappell, and played, note perfect, music by Liszt, Chopin, Beethoven and Schubert. He could also perform and improvise on any hymn. During a performance, which sometimes took up to an hour, sweat poured down his intense face. He mopped his forehead with a handkerchief and somehow managed to adjust his wig, which slipped to one side, while maintaining his furious pace at the keyboard.

His great love, apart from entertaining on the piano, was playing the trombone with the Regent's Hall Salvation Army band on a Sunday afternoon before he went to evensong at Christ Church. By chance, my mother had taken me there to hear the music. Afterwards, she approached him. 'I knew it was you, Mr Barratt, when I watched you playing the Death March. Then I remembered someone saying that the service was conducted by Colonel Barratt and guessed he must be your father.'

'Mrs Grundy, it's not generally known at Christ Church that I play the trombone for the Salvation Army, so . . .'

My mother laughed. I knew she liked to know other people's secrets.

One Sunday evening at our house, after a virtuoso performance on the piano, Clifford Barratt was unable to contain himself any longer. He finished the Chopin and, sweating profusely, stood up and pointed at Mosley's picture on the mantelpiece. After he had adjusted his wig and stopped panting, he said, 'Mrs Grundy! How can you, as a Christian, support this man, the most anti-Jewish politician Britain has ever produced?'

My mother also stood up and I thought she was about to reveal Mr Barratt's secret trombone playing, but instead she delivered her opening serve. 'Mosley's not anti-Jewish,' she said. 'The Jews are anti-Mosley.'

They stood facing each other. Then Mr Barratt sat down again on the piano stool and she sat down at the large, highly polished table, which was in the middle of the front room. For a few minutes it became a staring competition and the loser was the one who blinked first.

The rector intervened. 'Come, Mrs Grundy, surely you have read your own leader's speeches. You're always telling me to read them in his books.' He produced a notebook and I looked over his shoulder. It certainly wasn't his writing, which was small and untidy. He said it was a telegram that The Leader had sent to a man called Julius Streicher in May 1935. Mr Streicher had congratulated Mosley on making a brilliant speech. The Leader was naturally pleased and had sent back a telegram which the rector read aloud: ' "Please accept my best thanks for your kind telegram which greeted my speech in Leicester. It was received while I was away in London. I value your advice greatly in the midst of our hard struggle. The power of Jewish corruption must be destroyed in all countries before peace and justice can be successfully achieved in Europe. Our struggle to this end is hard but our victory is certain." ' On the same piece of paper was written in the rector's handwriting, '. . . above the stink of oil rises the stink of the Jew' and printed alongside it, 'Mosley to Mussolini after the latter's invasion of Abyssinia'.

The rector gave me the piece of paper. 'Keep that, Trevor, because one day you'll know why I'm talking like this. I know you don't at the moment because you're so young.'

I felt terribly hurt and insulted. After all, I was eleven years old and at Archbishop Tenison's and I had read all of Mosley's books, well, not *The Alternative*, which was really hard, but certainly the other books which were on the bookshelf. They were next to the only children's book I had ever read, Anna Sewell's *Black Beauty*.

Then Mr Cooper asked my mother how, as a Christian and a regular churchgoer, she could support a man who wrote in *Tomorrow We Live* that the Jew was an alien presence in Europe. He opened his notebook: ' "The Jew comes from the Orient and physically, mentally and spiritually, is more alien to us than any Western nation. There are many waste places of the Earth possessing great potential fertility and

66

the collective wisdom of a new Europe should be capable of finding territory where the Jews can escape the curse of no nationality." '

He passed me this piece of paper, too. I folded it up and put it in the prayer book which my father had given me on the day I was confirmed at St George's Chapel, opposite Lord's Cricket Ground.

It seemed that the three men from Christ Church had worked out a plan of attack and next it was the turn of Mr Barratt, who asked, 'How can a man who would like to lead the people of the British Empire, with its different races, religions and beliefs, have written in the same book, Mrs Grundy, that the Jews constitute a state within the nation and, I quote, "set the interests of their co-racialists at home and abroad above the interests of the British state"?

'Mrs Grundy,' he continued, 'Benjamin Disraeli was a Jewish Prime Minister of Great Britain and one of the best we ever had. Some of our best scientists are Jews, some of our greatest musicians. They don't put foreign interests before the interests of the people of this country. What I want to know is, does Mosley really believe what he says about the Jews or does he say it because he thinks it will make him popular with a certain type of person so he can gain power by teaching people to hate minorities?'

My mother rose, gazing around the room with a studied Mosley-look on her face, and replied as I knew she would. 'But he was only talking about the Jews who put their own interests before the interests of the British people. The Leader says: "We do not attack Jews for what they are but for what they do." ' She sat down, stood up and then sat down again. She looked at the three men and her eyes sparkled. Then she gave a smile of triumph first to Lovene, then to me. And I thought as I had thought so many times before that she was magnificent, a goddess, a totally indestructible person.

'Did he love Hitler?' She was performing like Mosley in front of the microphone. She answered her own question. 'He did. But then you should know, Rector, and you, Mr Cooper, that if you really love a man who is despised the world will hate you, perhaps crucify you. Mosley said, "Hitler was my friend" and if a man like Mosley can say Hitler was my friend, that's good enough for me.'

Mr Barratt said he could no longer listen to such nonsense. 'I don't see how you can claim to be a Christian while supporting such a terrible man, a Jew-hater and a man who had dozens of other women while he was still married to his first wife. And a lot of people say she was half-Jewish. Everyone in your Movement spends so much time covering up the past, covering up the truth. And then Sir Oswald, your beloved leader, stole Diana Guinness from her first husband when she was little more than a child, only twenty-two. What happened to her two children?' He reached for his overcoat and the two clerics rose. Before he left, Mr Barratt peered at the Christmas card on the mantelpiece. 'I love your card of Sir Oswald, Diana Mosley and their two children. But where are the children from their other marriages? What sort of example would those two set Christians in England if Sir Oswald and his black-shirted hooligans come to power?'

My mother looked at him as if he were a worm. 'When I listen to people like you, Clifford Barratt, on the subject of morality and Christian love I want to get a gin bottle and swing round the lamppost outside Christ Church when you're leaving a service. What did Jesus say? Jesus said, "Let him without sin cast the first stone." You, Clifford Barratt, you have got plenty of stones in your pocket.'

The 40 Blandford Square discussion group ended abruptly as the front door opened and my father's solid footsteps came up the echoey stairs. He entered the room red-faced and asked whether I had done my homework.

'Play chess with your father while I make him something to eat.'

I sat opposite him at the kitchen table and heard the guests leave. There was a strong smell of beer on his breath and his face looked puffy, his eyes full of anger. The night before he had told us that he had a business partner, a bald man called Charlie Watts. My father had bought him a Leica from an American who had smuggled it out of Germany. My mother thought that Charlie Watts was a drunk and that any money they made would disappear in the Mitre.

I made my standard opening move and felt the tension rising. 'Those Christ Church people have been round again. Do they live here? Haven't they got homes? It's gone nine and I've hardly eaten and probably won't now unless it's beans on toast because everything else in the house has been consumed by that bloody rector and the curate. Now the organist as well! Next week it will be the scoutmaster, the cubmaster and half the bloody congregation, including those two cripples your mother feeds and gives money to.'

'Supper's ready, Daddy,' said Lovene. 'It's beans on toast.'

For a few minutes my parents sat facing one another across the table. He complained about the smell of smoke. She complained about the smell of beer.

He asked, 'Do these people live in my house when I'm not here? Why do they leave as soon as I come in?'

She waved a hand in front of her face as if to remove a vision, or a smell. 'Because you make it unbearable. You force them to leave with your manners, and you've been in the Mitre again with Charlie Watts.'

'Don't you tell me what to do, you bloody bitch!' There was a loud bang as he hit the wooden table with a clenched fist. He picked up his plate. 'Is this what you give the rector? Is it? Is this what you give him?' He moved closer as if he was going to make her eat the beans. 'Is this what you give your bloody boyfriend . . . '

My father saw me staring. He stopped talking, swallowed his tea and I heard him half run down the stairs and the front door close.

Before I went to bed I touched the glass which covered Sir Oswald's face. 'Please, Sir Oswald, make them stop it. Come to London and do a campaign and make them stop fighting.'

The following week the same thing happened but it was much worse.

My father returned at nine o'clock. The Christ Church entourage had already departed. Lovene and I left my parents alone and my sister said something which hurt and puzzled me. 'I think they enjoy this,' she said.

My father told my mother in a soft, gentle voice that he had lost his Hampton Court pitch. 'The '43 Group said if I go back I'll get razored. They knew me from Speakers' Corner and Ridley Road.'

Then he shouted, 'We're going to be penniless again. It will be like Brighton, only worse. Ten times worse!'

Lovene and I stiffened. I heard a smacking sound. I opened the kitchen door and pleaded, 'Daddy, stop it! Please stop it, Daddy!'

My father stared at me. My mother had the breadknife in her hand. He was red and sweating and had his hands out as if he was going to throttle her. My mother's body was frozen as if she was posing for one of his pictures.

One of the flat doors above slammed and my mother put the knife back into the drawer. Lovene came in and put her arms around my mother's shoulders. She was silent, like an animal about to be beaten. My father left the room and my mother said to me, 'Go and play chess with him.'

As I set up the chess board I tried in vain to hide the tears running down my face. 'Why are you crying?' he snarled. 'Be a man. Do you hear me? Don't snivel. Be a man!'

I looked away towards the mantelpiece and said to myself, because the rector and Mr Cooper promised that prayers worked, 'Please, Sir Oswald, *please*.'

My father lost his pitch but got a job as a dark-room assistant after writing to a box number advertised in the *Evening News*. He started work on a Monday morning and was back home again by the afternoon. I heard him tell my mother that the boss was a Jew who had recognised him from the days in Ridley Road immediately after the foundation of Union Movement in 1948. He had been dismissed.

My mother telephoned the company and said she wanted to leave the address of her husband who was owed a day's pay. She told us at supper that the owner was Irish and had said my father knew only the most basic dark-room work and was no use.

After a few months on the dole, my father started work at Paddington telephone exchange as a switchboard operator. He worked mostly at night and left Blandford Square at five thirty with a Lilo air bed under one arm, sandwiches and a heavy book about history, religion or philosophy under the other. When he turned the corner there was no one to give him an encouraging Fascist salute.

He said to my mother, 'It's not so bad when the supervisor goes for his supper break. Then I can switch off and read. That way I survive until the morning. But in a way it's worse than prison. At least in prison you know you're going to get out.'

One evening I returned home from school after a violin lesson to find my father in the kitchen cleaning his bicycle, which he'd placed upside-down on the table. Bonnie, our fox terrier, was asleep underneath it. While wiping the rims with a cloth and oiling the chain, he told me that my mother and Lovene had left. Without looking at me he said, 'I suppose they've gone to live in some dump off King's Cross or Euston. You're staying here with me, so get yourself washed and do your homework. Get on with maths, not that religion stuff you're always doing, and we'll go for a walk before supper. Don't start snivelling for your mother. We're on our own and that's for the best, so be a man.'

I washed at the sink and sat down at the table in the front room. I heard him breathing heavily. I thought he was going to speak to me but he didn't. All he said was, 'This house is filthy. Dirt everywhere, from top to bottom.'

I could hear him take the bike down and push it backwards and forwards to test the brakes, which made Bonnie wake up.

'Your mother was always more interested in dressing up and parading round Regent's Park than doing the housework. And Lovene is getting just like her. How old is she . . . Lovene?'

'Seventeen,' I called back, trying to sound like a man not a weed. 'Seventeen, going on eighteen.'

'And you need toughening up. You're a real Mammie's boy. She used to put lipstick and rouge on you, do you remember that?' Then he stopped speaking, put on Bonnie's lead and said with great sadness in his voice, 'But then I was, too.'

It was a silent walk. After supper he put my black bike without a crossbar onto the table. 'I may as well sell this and get you a new one,' he said. 'You've had it for years.' He started cleaning, looking down, rubbing hard, muttering *filthy* this and *filthy* that.

I went in to say goodnight and hoped he wouldn't kiss me. He didn't, but as I stood there I was suddenly very afraid and felt goose-pimples everywhere. Without looking up, he spun the front wheel of my bike and said, 'Your mother was a prostitute. She used to go with men and take money. Her rotten mother and father, those damned Maurice people, used to get half of it and that evil old bastard Maurice would gamble it away on the horses. He'd lost everything and they'd have been living on the street if it hadn't been for your mother being pushed to that man Lawes in Whitley Bay when she was sixteen, younger than your sister is now. But he only wanted her because of her looks and dropped her like a hot potato when something better came along. Your stupid mother thought he was going to marry her, but you know what that bloody man Lawes did? When his wife died in Whitley Bay he sent her a card with a picture of lilies of the valley on it and inside a pound note and a message saying that he was getting married again and it was to a rich widow old enough to be his mother. And your mother wanted to kill herself but those damned Maurice people told her to go to London and make some money. And she had nothing but her looks. Nothing but her looks.'

He spun the wheel of the bike again and said, 'This wheel's wonky.'

I knelt down so I wouldn't have to look at him or acknowledge what I'd heard. I played with Bonnie, who rolled over so I could tickle her stomach.

When the spinning stopped he said, 'When she came back up north she was treated like a gypsy and if it hadn't been for me she'd have died in a room somewhere in London. That's what happens to them. But I married her and I sometimes think she only turned to Mosley to get revenge on her own people for doing what they did to her. What pretence! What hypocrisy, those bloody Maurices! They dressed her up and put a cross round her neck. And now she's making a fool of herself again, this time with that damned rector. She thinks if she leaves me he'll come running after her but he won't and I know why. He's in love with that woman who teaches Mr Cooper Hebrew at Church House. What's her name? Mrs Simpson? And your mother doesn't know it but Mrs Simpson's Jewish. She's making such a damned fool of herself.' A terrible smile crossed his face. 'A Jewess with a cross round her neck.' And then slowly and terrifyingly, 'That should please your mother.'

He spun the wheel hard and suddenly stopped it and spat out through the spokes, 'Get to bed! You shouldn't be listening to this.'

I went to bed and pulled the blanket up over my head and prayed that I would not wake up until my mother and Lovene had come home.

But before I went to sleep I climbed out of bed and wrote on a blank piece of paper in my religious affairs exercise book 'prostitute'. I wasn't exactly sure what it meant but it was something like a loose woman. Jesus had met a prostitute who loved Him and she was with Him when He died. And she was the first person to see Him when He rose again from the dead.

4

'Is that you, Trevor?'

I put my satchel, violin case and Bible down by the side of my bed and looked at my father through the crack in the door which divided my room from the kitchen.

He was jacketless and slumped in a chair with Bonnie on his lap. The dog heard me, jumped down and wagged.

'Fox terriers are more loyal than people,' said my father. 'When did you see Lovene and your Mam?'

'I saw them this morning before I went to school. They're staying at Church House. They sleep in a spare room above the rector and Mr Cooper.'

'I knew it.'

He told me to get on with my maths and listen to the wireless. He said he was going to have a drink with a friend, but I knew he was lying because he hadn't got a friend. He put on his jacket. I knew where he was off to. My stomach knotted.

Later, Ginger Griffiths from the choir told me what happened. Ginger was leaving Church House when my father arrived. He knocked on the door and rang the bell. When there was no immediate reply, he banged heavily on it and, as Ginger opened it, he stumbled inside but did not fall. He walked straight past Ginger and up the stairs to another door, which led to the rector's flat. Ginger said he looked drunk. He rang the bell and Mr Cooper appeared.

'Where's my wife?' Ginger heard him shout. Once Ginger knew something, all the choir would know and then the whole of Christ Church. When he told me the story I went crimson with embarrassment, the sort of uncontrollable blush that returns to haunt you for years afterwards.

Mr Cooper had tried to shut the door. Ginger heard him say, 'Mr Grundy, I'll be forced to call the police,' and then, 'You have no right . . . ' Ginger reported no further noise after that.

Later, Mr Cooper was seen holding a handkerchief to his nose, but the police were never called. I thought, 'Mr Cooper really believes in God because Jesus didn't call the police when he was attacked by the Jews in the Garden of Gethsemane.'

Later that night, my father returned home, put his arms around me and kissed me on the forehead. It is the only time I can remember him kissing me. 'This has been bad for you,' he said. 'Your mam and Lovene are coming home tomorrow. Your mam has promised. We have both promised that this will never happen again.'

Then he sat down and read the *Evening News*, as if that was that. The paper rustled and I saw Bonnie jump onto his lap. I went next door to try to do my homework but the maths problems were impossible and I cried until I could no longer see the page.

Later, he called me for supper and smiled as if he was really happy.

'Newcastle won but Sunderland . . . beaten again. I give up! Don't know why I support the silly buggers. They need a decent goalkeeper. Why can't they buy Manchester City's Bert Trautmann? There's a real goalkeeper. Ex-paratrooper with the Luftwaffe. That's what Sunderland need between the posts but I suppose the so-called managers at Roker Park won't touch him because he's German. As for Arsenal, lucky home win. Dirtiest team in the first division, Arsenal.'

When the notice appeared on the board at school showing who had gone up to 3A and 3B, I was shocked. My name was not among them, even though I had come third out of thirty-one in 2C. My housemaster, Mr Griffiths, said that although my maths was hopeless I had worked hard and he was also surprised I had not been pushed up a stream, but there was nothing he could do about it.

On my mother's advice, I asked to see Dr Robinson, the head-master, and as I waited nervously outside his office I overheard his secretary say, 'Trevor Grundy, ex-2C' and the name 'Father Spencer'.

I stood in front of the headmaster, trembling, which was a tradition at Archbishop Tenison's in the 1950s.

'You're the boy whose parents were going to divorce,' he said, as three boys from the form above me were leaving his room. 'Let me see.' He scrutinised the file without looking at me. 'Your father had applied earlier this year for you to be transferred to Morpeth Grammar School, so he could go and live with his father . . . your grandmother died last year . . . Where is it? Some place near Newcastle . . . Ellington Village.' He took off his glasses and peered at me as if I was an insect pinned to a board. 'You take no interest in sport. You have shown no desire to join the Air Training Corps and the only thing you're good at is religion. The PT instructor says that you're unable to get over the wooden horse, stand on your head, or carry the medicine ball more than a few yards. And you want to take up fencing. Why fencing? Because the other boys don't want to do it, perhaps?

'I have been headmaster here for twenty-three years and Tenison's has never yet seen a boy pass religion at O level, let alone A level. And your maths is hopeless. What do you think you're going to do in life with religion, biology and history, without maths, Latin, French or another modern language? Well, you're going to stay in the C stream. Indeed, you're lucky to be at a grammar school. Perhaps this time next year there'll be a review.'

That night I asked my mother why the rector had been to see Dr Robinson.

'He thought it might help, being a vicar,' she said. 'He knows how much you wanted to go up a class. Well, I think your headmaster is stupid. If you're going to be a vicar, what's the best subject? Religion. And what do you want to join the Air Training Corps for? Drop bombs on the Germans? Far better you drop bombs on Mrs Simpson!'

It was the first time I had heard her mention the Hebrew teacher's name.

The relationship between my mother and father appeared to have improved. There were fewer rows, none of them violent. My father had decided that he would always work nights at Paddington exchange and, instead of sleeping during the day, learn The Knowledge, which would qualify him for a licence to drive a black Hackney cab.

'They make a fortune,' I heard him tell my mother. 'I know one man who makes twenty pounds a day and only pays tax on nine pounds a week.'

The kitchen became a kind of map command post and the limitless energy he might have put into theology when he was a young man now went into learning every street and route in London. 'You should be doing this,' he said to me. 'When you leave school, we could get a couple of cabs and form a company, Grundy and Son.'

The *Marylebone Mercury* carried a short announcement on an inside page. There was a picture of the rector of Christ Church, the Reverend Christopher John Edward Spencer, and his intended, Mrs Pat Simpson, a widow who lectured in religion and Hebrew studies at the University of London. They were to marry later in 1952.

In the kitchen I sat silently next to my mother, who was transfixed by the announcement. She looked like one of the waxworks in Madame Tussauds. My father came in that morning, I thought quite cheerily. I think my mother remained in that chair, her face white and waxy, for most of the day.

After supper she said she wanted to speak to me alone, without my father or Lovene, so we went to Regent's Park and walked to Queen Mary's Gardens in the Inner Circle.

'The rector has been hypnotised by this woman,' she said. 'How can a Christian vicar marry a Jewess? What will happen to their children? They'll be half-Jewish, or what's the rector going to do, drain their blood?'

She showed me a letter she had received from him that day. It was written on Christ Church headed notepaper.

Dear Mrs Grundy,

Naturally, I hope you and Sidney and Lovene and Trevor will come to the wedding.

Sincerely,

Chris Spencer

She told me to ring Church House to make an appointment to see him, to tell him he had betrayed Jesus by marrying a Jew and that none of us would go to his wedding. She said that we would also have to leave Christ Church and that I would, of course, leave the choir. We would attend for the final time that Sunday and, if anyone asked why we were leaving, we would tell them that the rector had betrayed Jesus.

She said we should be getting back because it was my father's night off and we were going to the pictures at the Odeon in Edgware Road to see a film about Rommel, starring James Mason.

I dreaded the thought of going to the Odeon with them. I knew my father would be passing comments throughout the film and, with a rector/Jewess marriage coming up, he would get my mother's full support. I imagined the evening before us. 'Jewish propaganda,' he'd say loudly, when the credits appeared on the screen at the end of the film. 'Look at that, Edna: Silverstein, Davids, Isaacson.' People in the front rows would turn round and glare at him but that only ever acted as a spur. 'Rubinstein. Look who wrote the music, Wolffers . . . my God, not a gentile name in sight and it's supposed to be a film about Rommel.'

The following day, the Grundy family received a letter from the London Diocese of the Anglican Church which informed us that, as regular churchgoers, we had been chosen to represent Christ Church in a competition to find Marylebone's 'Christian Family of the Year'. The Bishop of London would deliver a sermon and prizes would be handed out at a ceremony in St John's Wood the following month.

My mother said she would have to write back and explain why we had decided to leave Christ Church. My father said he couldn't have gone anyway, because he was on nights.

Later that week, I faced the rector in his study. He had a handsome face and I loved him like a father.

He poured some tea and lit a cigarette. 'Why won't you come to the wedding?'

'Because you're a leader of the Church. Because you're supposed to be setting everyone an example and you're going to marry a Jewess, and the Jews killed Jesus.'

'Is that what you really think, or is it what someone else has told you to say?'

'It's what I really think.'

'You can't know how cruel you're being. It's terrible what you've been made to say. You're too young to say such things.'

'Jesus was only twelve or thirteen when he argued with the priests about things he thought were wrong.'

The rector looked at me and said, 'It's high time you learnt, Trevor Grundy, that you are not Jesus Christ.'

He put his arm around me but I moved away. 'You have become like a son to me. Give Pat – give Mrs Simpson – a chance. She's a wonderful woman, very clever, and I'm sure that one day, despite this cruelty, she will learn to like you, even love you.'

'If you have children, they will be half-Jewish.'

'They will be Christians, Trevor. Not gentile, not Jewish but Christians.'

I blurted it out. 'What are you going to do? Drain their blood?' I wanted to cry. I did not want to lose this man from my life. But even worse was the thought of losing my mother's approval.

I had to tell Mr Barratt that I would be leaving the choir. The rector had already told him why so he said nothing, just put his hand on my shoulder and gave me a sort of pat. I would sing at only one more service.

That last Sunday at Christ Church my mother sat on her own in the middle of the church. Lovene had refused to go with her and said she

79

would definitely go to the rector's wedding, even if she had to leave home and live at a civil service hostel.

For the first time, my sister and I were becoming strangers. Lovene was moving towards semi-independence and was increasingly critical of my mother's curt dismissals of those who didn't see the world her way. I was, more and more, an appendage of my mother. More than ever, I could not conceive of arguing with her, of losing her love and support.

As the service reached its climax, the rector and Mr Cooper prepared the bread and the wine as the server's bell rang. I looked up from the front row of the choir and studied the oil painting hanging over the altar. I thought, 'But everyone I love is here.'

Then my soprano voice rang out through the church:

> O lamb of God
> That taketh away the sins of the world
> Have mercy upon us.
>
> O lamb of God
> That taketh away the sins of the world
> Grant us Thy peace.

The confirmed in the congregation walked to the altar and knelt at the rail as the rector held the host above his head.

When my mother returned to her seat she looked as if she had lost her soul.

My father must have been particularly grateful that Mr Cooper never called the police that night when he went drunk to the rectory, or filed a complaint against him, because shortly after my thirteenth birthday I was escorted to the headmaster's office by a worried-looking housemaster.

'I don't know what you've done, Grundy, but the headmaster is furious and there are two plain-clothes policemen waiting to see you in his room.'

I knew what I'd done. To impress the school rebel, Charles

Caldwell, I had taken my father's Luger to school inside my violin case, like a mafioso in Chicago. Caldwell had dismissed me as a violin-playing, religious twerp.

This took place not long after the Craig–Bentley case, where Christopher Craig, the teenage son of a bank official, received a life sentence, later reduced, for shooting a policeman, and his unarmed associate, Derek Bentley, was hanged. Bentley was below normal intelligence, illiterate and an epileptic. The hanging sparked off a spate of social protest and changed the image of the police force. They were no longer beyond criticism in Britain and Caldwell had said he'd love to kill a cop.

The chief witness, a policeman's son, was brought into Dr Robinson's office. He said he had seen me show Caldwell the gun in the biology lab, which overlooked the main hall. Frightened as I was, I wanted to laugh. Did they think Caldwell was going to point the gun through one of the windows and shoot Punch, assassinate the head?

Dr Robinson was speechless. His main concern was that there would be no mention of the incident in the local newspaper. He greatly cared for the school's reputation as a symbol of the Establishment and the Church of England and was terrified of adverse publicity.

The detectives looked at me carefully. One said, 'Where did you get this gun from, sonny?'

I told him.

'So it's your father's gun. Probably picked it up in Germany after the war, did he? Good job it wasn't loaded.'

'Has your father got more weapons at home?' asked the other policeman.

'No, sir,' I replied. 'Just the Luger but he never takes it out of the sideboard or the room. Honest to God, he doesn't. I'm very sorry. He won't get into trouble, will he?'

'He will if it's not licensed,' came the reply.

That night my father hit me for the first and only time. He was furious. 'You've made me look like a bloody fool and they've taken the gun away from me. You must be mad taking it to school.' Then he hit me across the head.

'Don't! Sidney!' shouted my mother. 'It's not his fault. You shouldn't have a gun in the house.'

Later that week a representative from Special Branch who knew my father's political background came to the house and had a cup of tea with us. His job was to keep an eye on 'fringe movements'. I heard him say, 'Well, Sid, I'm going to have to put all this on your file but we've never regarded Sir Oswald as a fringe leader and he's always co-operated with the police. But you've got to be more careful. You shouldn't have let your kid have access to a drawer with a gun in it.'

My father was never charged and the gun was never mentioned again. But the matter did not end there.

Dr Robinson called me downstairs the next morning. With him was the senior history teacher, a man called Birchenough, who had a tiny moustache and wore his hair like Adolf Hitler.

Dr Robinson looked at me. 'You have disgraced your teachers, you have disgraced me and you have disgraced Archbishop Tenison's Grammar School. Under normal circumstances I would expel you, but taking into account your recent problems, we have decided to give you one more chance, Grundy.'

The following Friday, Dr Robinson went to the lectern and read from the Sermon on the Mount. As soon as he had crossed himself quickly, he shouted out the caning list. My name was called and in front of the school I received six strokes, delivered by Birchenough. Between strokes, Caldwell told me, Birchenough brushed aside his lock of hair, just as Hitler had when he'd got excited during a speech at Nuremburg. I wondered how the headmaster of a Christian school could watch with a smile on his face as boys were beaten. Jesus told us to forgive, not seven times but seventy times seven: the Bible said that vengeance was the Lord's, that we should turn the other cheek when attacked or wronged.

That night I told my mother that I no longer wanted to be a vicar but I didn't tell her about the caning. If being a Christian leader meant emulating Dr Punch, I'd sooner change my vocation. Better to be a Caldwell than a Birchenough, I smarted.

Later, I heard her say to my sister, 'I think he's fallen for some lass. The next thing we know, she'll be pregnant. And what will happen then? It will be the end of everything. Who told him about sex? I certainly didn't.'

In 1955 James Dean scowled at the world's youth, while Brigitte Bardot sparked off frenetic wanking competitions in the back row of form 5C.

Before classes or between classes, two or more boys would produce from their satchels magazines containing pictures of Brigitte Bardot, Marilyn Monroe or Jane Russell and the first one to ejaculate won the bet which might amount to several shillings, most of it gambled lunch money. The winner was usually a disgusting boy with blond hair and red eyes. He'd grin and say, 'I win because I've got the best pictures of BB.'

Boys of my age group left school at four o'clock. When we got about a hundred yards from the school front gates we took off our caps and remoulded our hair. Some tried for a James Dean look; others, me included, went for a Tony Curtis. All of us combed our head carefully at the back to resemble a duck's arse, a DA. One Friday morning, Birchenough announced that if he caught anyone with a 'DA' or a 'Tony Curtis' he'd cane that boy every morning for a week. Dr Punch nodded in agreement, delighted, it seemed, at the thought of more mass whackings on the school stage.

Most members of my form had made up their minds to leave Tenison's as soon after their fifteenth birthdays as possible. They were either going to enter the print as apprentices or join the Royal Air Force. I didn't have a clue what I wanted to do so it seemed that the best course of action was to stay on, take my O levels and see what happened next. I might get English, history, geography, biology and religion. Maths was an impossibility. I'd received zero during the mock exams, which must remain an unbeaten record at Tenison's.

So when school finally broke up for the summer holidays in 1955, I said goodbye to almost everyone I knew. A group of 5C scholars, without an O level between them, waited for Birchenough to come out of the main door at four thirty. One shouted, 'Hey, Birchy, you can't do anything to us now!' and they turned their backs on him, revealing magnificent DAs. The flustered caner quickened his step to the bus stop.

That summer, the secretary of Union Movement, Alf Flockhart, came to the house to ask my mother if she would do him a favour. Mosley was a friend of many of the surviving Nazi leaders and some of them wanted their sons and daughters to travel to London to meet people of their own age and study English. Would the Grundys put up some of the young Germans? Naturally, my mother would be paid for doing this. She willingly agreed and gave the impression that she would accommodate a division of the Waffen SS at 40 Blandford Square if The Leader requested it.

After a beer with my father, Alf Flockhart said that it was time I started doing something for Mosley and Union Movement. He said he'd been told that I'd had a wonderful singing voice before my voice broke. 'If you can sing for the church, surely you can speak for Mosley,' he said.

'Speak about what?' I asked.

'About the aspirations, the hopes and dreams of young people. You're young, aren't you?'

I was beginning to wonder, for my life seemed much too sober, unexciting and cold-blooded. But then our first German house guest arrived and it suddenly became very clear that I was as hot-blooded a teenager as my classmates.

Waltraut Skorzeny was the daughter of Otto 'Scarface' Skorzeny, who rescued Benito Mussolini from the partisans towards the end of the war. Skorzeny was a master of guerrilla warfare and one of Hitler's most decorated soldiers.

Waltraut was seventeen, a honey blonde, athletically built and very tanned. She had beautiful blue eyes, strong white teeth and a firm jaw. She had large breasts.

I'd seen dozens of girls just like Waltraut in my father's Second

World War books. Captions described them as 'Germany's mothers of the future'. Many of the pictures had been taken by Hitler's favourite photographer, Leni Riefenstahl. She specialised in pictures of Waltraut-type girls throwing their bodies and right arms out in the direction of Hitler as he passed by in a car. I asked Lovene, 'Why don't we have girls like that throwing their arms out at Mosley?' She looked at me with disgust.

Waltraut's English was reasonable but it was the way she said words such as 'please', 'thank you' and 'excuse me' that so excited me. She pursed her lips and pouted like Brigitte Bardot.

She was in London to try to find the right college to prepare her for the Cambridge English Exam, so she could qualify for a job as a translator. Waltraut was also studying French, Spanish, Italian and Russian. She said that one day Germany would conquer the Soviet Union and interpreters would be required.

When Waltraut arrived I was so overawed all I could think of to say was, 'You're very brown.' I said the words slowly, mesmerised by her magnificent breasts.

'You don't speak any German?' she said, hardly acknowledging my presence. 'My father owns several large companies. He is a personal friend of President Franco and I live part of the year in Madrid and part of the year in Bavaria. That's why I am brown. I also ski, swim and walk a great deal in the hills and the mountains.'

After I had walked her round Regent's Park, shown her the ducks and swans, and received stares from several Jewish ladies who had seen a Waltraut or two during their days in Germany or Eastern Europe, she said to me, 'Please comb your hair. I am embarrassed to be in the middle of London with someone who is trying to look like a Hollywood actor.'

Each night I'd lie awake and think of the German Valkyrie who'd taken over my freshly decorated bedroom.

I'd been relegated to a small, white-washed room next to my father's dark-room, but that was of no concern to a fifteen-year-old boy who found himself deeply in love. Waltraut was the best looking girl in the world and she was sleeping in my bed! I found it easy to follow The Leader's recommendation that we should love our European comrades, especially the Germans.

One evening, when my parents had gone out, Waltraut and I were left alone in the front room. My sister had lent me a long-playing record with Tchaikovsky's *Italian Caprice* on it. I put it on and Waltraut and I hummed the theme. At the end of the record, I tried to kiss her. She put her hand across her face and said, 'Trevor, please don't be a silly little boy. I have a very large boyfriend in Germany who is twenty-two years old and he would not enjoy it if I tell him that an English *Halbstarker* had tried to kiss me.' I asked her what the German word meant and she said it referred to someone who was half-strong or half-grown-up.

The following week she left for Bavaria or Spain or wherever it was and I was delighted to get my room back and put my hair into a Tony Curtis again. At fifteen, it's amazing how fast you can fall out of love.

The rest of the German invaders followed later that year.

Next, we had a six-feet-tall sixteen-year-old called Klaus Naumann, son of the former Brownshirt officer who served as Under-secretary of State in Germany's wartime Propaganda Ministry. Klaus's father had been named in Hitler's will as Dr Goebbels's successor. He'd been the last person to talk to Goebbels before the family suicide in the bunker, shortly after the death of Hitler and Eva Braun.

During the three weeks Klaus stayed with us I cannot remember him smiling once.

Alf Flockhart told my mother, 'He suffered badly in 1945 because the Russians destroyed the family house and he and his mother had to scrounge from dustbins. It was common after the war. Most German women were raped by Russian soldiers.'

I introduced Klaus to my friend Timothy Adams, who was even taller than Klaus. Tim had thick, brown, curly hair and large facial features. He had won a scholarship to the prestigious London public school, Haberdashers Askes, and I was seeing less and less of him, but still counted him as my best and oldest friend.

Tim was a brilliant sportsman and in particular a magnificent spin-bowler. We decided to teach Klaus how to play cricket. We used a real cricket ball, not the tennis or rubber ball demanded by the uniformed park-keepers. Klaus swung my Donald Bradman bat around as if he were an American teenager with a baseball bat. He kept missing the ball and Timothy laughed at the German's antics in front of the wicket.

'Why are you laughing you . . . you . . . you . . . '

'Come on, Klaus,' I said, as if I were talking to a boy from Tenison's. 'It's only a game. It's only a game of cricket. Not to be taken seriously.'

Klaus went red in the face. 'I don't like this stupid game and I don't like this stupid country.' He threw the bat down, walked home and the following day told Alf Flockhart that he wanted money to return to Germany.

Klaus lacked the charm of Gertrude Himmler. She appeared one day at 40 Blandford Square with Jeffrey Hamm and Bob Row, a tall, open-faced Lancastrian who had been appointed editor of *Union*. Fraulein Himmler, as we'd been told to call her, was visiting London for the first time and Mosley had suggested that she should be introduced to some leading Movement members, hence the visit to the Grundys.

As Bob and Jeffrey put their hands out to help Fraulein Himmler from the taxi, Mrs Adams and Timothy, in his Haberdashers Askes blazer and cap, walked past. My mother said, 'Oh, Mrs Adams, may I introduce you to a German friend of ours, Fraulein Himmler. And this is Timothy, Mrs Adams's son, Fraulein Himmler.'

Fraulein Himmler smiled but said nothing. She looked like a schoolteacher, with fair hair, National Health-style glasses, a tweed skirt and brown jacket. She obviously knew she was a very, very, important person as far as we were concerned.

The adults disappeared into the house and I stayed outside, too young to converse with such an eminent person. After half an hour, Fraulein Himmler came out, smiled at me and touched my face with her left hand, before being driven off with Jeffrey and Bob Row in the taxi, which had waited for her.

Later, my mother told me that Fraulein Himmler had told her that her father was a great man, a very misunderstood man whose reputation had been destroyed by the Jews. My mother told her how Mr Grundy had been taken away by the British secret service and thrown into prison because 'he refused to fight our German brothers in a Jewish quarrel'.

The following day, Timothy and I were kicking a tennis ball around opposite the convent walls in Harewood Avenue when he asked why my family had so many German friends. 'My parents often ask why you're always entertaining Germans. My father says that it's a pity any of them are still alive after what they did in the war.'

'What did they do in the war that we didn't do?' I asked.

'We didn't kill Jews. My father said Hitler and his henchmen killed millions of Jews. If Hitler had got his chance he'd have killed my mother and grandmother. They're Jews, you know. My father's from Ireland but my mother's an English Jew, so I'm half-Jewish.' And with that he picked up the ball, put it in his pocket and walked back to his home without saying goodbye.

When I told my mother that night, she said, 'It doesn't surprise me at all. Mrs Adams and her mother have a Jewish look about them and Timothy is looking more and more foreign. But you never know with those people. He's gone to a Jewish school and she's probably told him to say that to get on with the other boys, I bet.'

I felt sad and confused for some time. How could this person I'd been proud to call my friend for so many years be a Jew? Tim and I had been growing apart anyway, partly because I was just at a grammar school and he was at a public school and he was an excellent sportsman and the most I'd ever scored at cricket was three not out because of rain. But now, I supposed, I was meant to hate him. The boy I'd called my best friend . . . And weren't Jews meant to be evil? Yet I'd loved him as a brother. My head spun in confusion. I wondered how it was that the person I'd really disliked was Klaus and he was German, and yet my mother said that I was supposed to love him because he was a fellow Aryan brother and had scoured dustbins looking for crusts after the war. After my treatment at the hands of

Waltraut and Klaus, I felt my mother had it all wrong. Better to be Tim than Klaus. But then where did that leave me as a supporter of Oswald Mosley, the man who had written so many books and articles and delivered so many speeches in London saying that the Germans were Britain's natural allies and that if the two great peoples of common stock could stop fighting and work together then Europe would become a paradise on earth?

After a few days with no further contact from Timothy or conversation with Mrs Adams, whose proud head now never turned towards the windows of 40 Blandford Square, I decided that it was best, as usual, to fall in line with my mother. Mosley must be right, because Mosley was always right, because he was Mosley.

5

The year 1956 brought the Hungarian Revolution and the Suez Crisis and Mosley was determined to make the most of the political turmoil. Mosley was sixty years old in 1956 but looked a lot younger. Twenty years earlier he had been at the height of his fame – or notoriety – as Britain's leading Fascist. That year he had marched at the head of 2,000 Blackshirts to Cable Street in the East End of London. They'd been met by almost 100,000 opponents, screaming abuse and the Spanish Civil War slogan, *They shall not pass.* Sensing bloodshed, the police had surrounded Mosley's column and asked him to turn round. He'd complied. It was a stunning defeat for the British Union of Fascists but its propagandists turned it into a significant victory by claiming that the Establishment and the police had caved in to the forces of Communism and lawlessness. Earlier that same year, on 18 June 1936, Mosley had been stoned in Manchester and six of his supporters were knocked unconscious as they defended him against attackers in Hull. In September, he was assailed by a shower of missiles at Holbeck Moor, Leeds, during a meeting which attracted a crowd of 30,000 people, and at Carfax Assembly Rooms in Oxford, Mosley had taunted his opponents and caused a riot by playing the Horst Wessel song on the gramophone before he started speaking.

In 1956, Mosley was still capable of rousing strong emotions. He remained a fiery speaker and an imposing figure. His supporters said that he was in 'good nick' and admired his Mediterranean tan and his familiar grey campaign suit with the missing button. Yet he now gave the impression that age had mellowed him and experience modified his opinions. He appeared the elder statesman.

On the platform, Mosley continued to be a brilliant performer, a magician with words, and around the dinner tables of fellow aristocrats he was said to be just as fascinating. He was considered one of the most intelligent and witty hosts in Europe, and at home, in France, we were told, Mosley's regular visitors still included the Duke and Duchess of Windsor.

Bob Row, the editor of *Union*, told me that his ambition when he retired was to write a play or a book about Mosley and the Duke talking and planning together in Paris during the 1950s. 'What a story. The man who could have been King of England with the man who could have been the Prime Minister!'

Bob was a frequent visitor to 40 Blandford Square. My mother adored him. 'How's The Leader?' she'd ask before he got his coat off. When he left, she'd say, 'It's like Paul visiting the Corinthians.'

Union came out on Thursday nights and Bob brought it round to our house and had supper. He'd sit for hours in the kitchen with my mother and Lovene while I read every word, hoping that one day I would become as great a writer as Bob. Many of his articles told readers just how right Mosley had been to oppose war in 1939. They were written in staccato sentences which ended with an exclamation mark. With time and training, I'd be able to write like that.

'He comes round to talk to me, I know that,' said my mother, 'but I think he quite likes Lovene and obviously thinks the world of Trevor.'

At the start of 1956 Bob told us that OM was going to make his big comeback because the Jews were trying to overthrow Nasser in Egypt. 'They'll go to war against Nasser, Mrs G, and Britain will go in with them because of that chinless wonder, Anthony Eden. We'll all be dragged into another Jewish war and British lives will be lost in the Middle East and the Arabs will turn away from Britain and look to the Soviet Union.' He said that one day Mosley's Britain and

Europe would make an alliance with the Soviets and when my mother expressed amazement he calmed troubled waters by saying that even the Russians had found out how awful the Jews were and Stalin had got rid of as many as Hitler.

He explained that the Soviet Union was the headquarters of the anti-Zionist movement and Mosley's Britain would prefer to side with the Russians than the Americans because there were more Jews in New York than in the whole of Israel. 'And if we attack Zionists no one can say we're anti-Jewish, can they Mrs G? Even some Jews are anti-Israel.'

Bob tucked into his beans on toast with a Cheshire-cat grin on his face, as if he'd just found the solution to a difficult crossword puzzle.

Although he looked at my mother when he spoke, it soon became obvious that his intention was to interest Lovene. They walked round the park, went to art galleries and Bob spent less time at 302 Vauxhall Bridge Road.

Meanwhile, The Leader packed halls throughout Britain – in Manchester, Birmingham and London – speaking sometimes for two hours and receiving thunderous applause. We travelled all over the country in coaches and, amazingly, there was hardly any fighting. There was rarely any mention of the meetings in the press: Mosley only received publicity when there was a scuffle. It infuriated Bob.

'Mrs G! We send out circulars to every news editor in Fleet Street about what OM's doing and saying but they only report him when there's been a fight. It makes me sick. They put a D-notice on OM after the war and told all the editors to boycott him. The BBC was the first to go along with the ban. Perhaps we should start Yid-bashing again and get some decent publicity in the press.'

As part of the new offensive, Diana Mosley started a literary magazine, the *European*, which was sold at 302. Her friends from Britain and France wrote for her. Henry Williamson made contributions and so did Richard Aldington, author of *Death of a Hero*, which Bob said he'd lend me. There were articles by Ezra Pound and several experts on Pound made contributions, including two men who appeared almost every month, Alan Neame and

Desmond Stewart, who'd met Mosley when they were students at Oxford University after the Second World War. Bob said, 'The Leader wants *Union* to win over the masses but he needs the *European* to pull in the intellectuals. OM knows who counts and who made all the sacrifices and those are the people who'll be rewarded first but we can't ignore the others. The intellectuals will come in at the very last moment. It happened in Germany, Mrs G. Then they all fawned on Hitler. Same thing will happen with OM.'

When Soviet tanks invaded Hungary at the end of 1956, Mosley told large audiences in London that Eden had given Khrushchev an excuse to go in and quell the student uprising, because how could the West condemn him when they had invaded Egypt? At times my mother became almost hysterical in the kitchen and said that we should drop all pretence and let everyone know we were supporters of the greatest man in British history who'd spent his entire life fighting Communism, which had at last shown itself in its true colours.

The night the tanks went into Budapest a group of us, including a tall slim boy with golden hair, an open-neck checked shirt and blue jeans whom I'd not met before went in a van around Paddington, Marble Arch, Kilburn and Marylebone and painted anti-Communist slogans on walls. Near Edgware Road, close to where Ginger Griffiths lived in a vast red-brick council estate, I held a bucket full of paint while the new boy drew a huge white flash and circle. I heard the noise of tyres on a wet road and then a voice.

'And what do you two little sods think you're up to, then?'

Two policemen looked down on me. One shone a torch into my face and then lit up the other boy. He squinted at the powerful light. He had a lovely face. He took hold of the policeman's torch and pushed it downwards.

'Don't shine that into my face,' he said, as if he was talking to a waiter.

I thought, 'God, we're going to be arrested,' and then, 'But perhaps it doesn't matter if my name gets into the *Mercury* because Mum said we can stop pretending.'

The golden boy said, 'This is our sign, officer. We're anti-Communist and we're protesting about students in Hungary being murdered on the streets of Budapest by Soviet tanks. We're students and all of us feel the same way.'

One of the policemen said, 'Well, you should have said.' They looked at one another and then told us to beat it. 'Take that bucket with you and don't let us catch you doing this again or there *will* be trouble.'

I went hurrying off into the night to tell the others what had happened.

'That boy with you was Max Mosley, OM's son,' said John Wood, who'd become increasingly active in the Movement now he'd returned from National Service and had digs in London. He came to the house with other young Union Movement supporters. They pretended it was to seek guidance from older members and talk about the old days before the war, but it was clear to me that John was infatuated with Lovene. My father took an immediate and extremely strong dislike to him. 'That phoney public school voice of his,' he said. 'Knew his mother and father. *La di da* this and *la di da* that.'

My mother snapped. 'They support The Leader. Do you want your only daughter to start going out with boys who *aren't* in the Movement?'

The following weekend about fifty Mosleyites joined a march after a massive rally in Trafalgar Square. The more experienced Movement members got to the front and said that we should go to Farringdon and protest outside the headquarters of the *Daily Worker*. Hundreds followed. When we got there, bricks were hurled through the newspaper office's windows. Within minutes, the police were on the spot and this time there was no tolerance or understanding about the anti-Communist nature of the attack.

One shouted, 'Get *that* little bastard,' and half a dozen of them went tearing after John, who was a skilful rugby player. He moved like lightning and we tried to keep up with him. We disappeared into the night and joined bus queues or stood looking into shop windows or walked to the nearest Underground and then met up again at

302 Vauxhall Bridge Road to compare notes. When we came out later that evening, a plain-clothes policeman said to Jeffrey Hamm. 'Try that stunt again and we'll close you down, do you hear me? One more time . . .'

Bob told us later that OM was delighted with what had happened. 'There's only one man with a consistent anti-Communist track record in England and that's The Leader, Mrs G. All the rest compromised and went trotting off to Moscow to have tea with Uncle Joe. Mrs Grundy, the people of Britain are waking up. They're seeing sense and they're turning to the one man who can save them.'

She echoed the words, 'The one man.'

Bob said the time was right for the formation of a youth wing and that I should lead it, or help form it, with other young men of my age. Until then I had kept a low profile at school, remembering that what happened at 40 Blandford Square was one thing and what happened outside was another. But after Hungary, nearly everyone under forty was anti-Communist, even those in the Communist and Labour Parties. I taught some of the boys a Movement song and they thought it was great. They sang it in the playground to the tune of the Labour Party's anthem. Even the masters laughed.

> *The red flag is turning pink,*
> *It's not so red as people think.*
> *With gallons of beer and gallons of blood,*
> *We'll drag the red flag through the mud.*

Bob waxed lyrical in *Union*. He wrote on the front page that at last the British people would turn to the man who had fought Communism on the streets of his own country.

I invited a small group of Tenisonians to a Mosley dinner at Victoria. A long-haired boy called Gaisford, whose only interest was getting to art college, said he'd come as he'd like to paint Mosley. Lawson, who bore an uncanny resemblance to Rudolf Hess, said that he wanted to read what Mosley had written before hearing him speak. 'I don't want to be swayed,' he said. Another classmate, Walters, said that he'd like to come because he liked beer and the Nazi party started in Munich at a beer festival, didn't it? They all said that someone had to stand up against Communism and Mosley might be the right man to follow, after all.

For the first time in my life I felt a part of my peer group. I no longer felt like an oddball. As Jeffrey Hamm had told my father long before, 'We *were* right and we *are* right.'

Movement dinners were held two or three times a year at a restaurant over a pub not far from Victoria Station. The licensee supported the pre-war BUF. His wife was Italian. She hated Mosley and said that Mussolini had destroyed Italy.

Dinners were attended by about one hundred and fifty to two hundred members and their guests. Bob told us that Jeffrey Hamm carefully scrutinised the list in case there were suspicious names, 'police spies,' he said. I hoped that my father would not repeat at this dinner what he had said at a previous Movement conference. The debate following The Leader's speech had turned to immigration. Members had said that too many West Indians were coming into Britain and that there'd be trouble.

My father rose and said that the problem wasn't the blacks, it was the Jews. Red-faced and with great passion he'd screamed, 'And if you're looking for the first man in Britain to turn on the gas taps, I'm here!' He hit his chest with a clenched fist and waited for applause. It did not come. He sat down, looked around several times and then looked at Mosley.

I watched The Leader's face. For a few moments he stared at my father and then Jeffrey Hamm went to him with a piece of paper and announced that we'd have a short break.

As we moved from our seats, a few old members slapped my father on the back. One said, 'Suppose you shouldn't have said that, Sid, but I would, too.'

There were always two toasts at Movement dinners, the first to Oswald Mosley, the second to Her Majesty The Queen. Men who had spent the best part of the war detained at His Majesty's pleasure leapt to their feet and toasted the health and long life of King George

VI's daughter, Elizabeth.

A collection was held after the meal and without fail my father would contribute twenty or twenty-five pounds, though he could ill afford it. The money went to Sanctuary Press to keep paying for the weekly *Union* or to help fund an election campaign in the East End. Mosley supporters always came bottom in council elections but there was always a candidate, always a rally, always a defeat.

'It's twenty-five pounds from the Grundy family, thank you, Sid and Edna.' My father got his round of applause and sat down beaming as the whisky and beer went down his throat. 'No, this is my round,' he said.

My mother looked at him. 'Careful, Sidney. Careful.'

Alf Flockhart raised a beer glass and shouted out, 'The Grundys.'

Members responded and Mosley smiled, his small eyes beaming in our direction.

'What a man!' said my mother. 'Look at him, Sidney. Look at him! What a man!'

The guest of honour in 1956 was Hans Ulrich Rudel, one of Hitler's most decorated pilots, who had shot down hundreds of Russian planes on the Eastern Front and who had lost his legs in the process. Mosley's Euphorion Books of Dublin published his book, *Stuka Pilot*, for twelve shillings and sixpence. It was a great success.

My Tenison friends and I shook hands with Rudel, who told us that the great English pilot, Captain Douglas Bader, had dropped him false legs when he heard about his accident on the Russian front. Lawson was incredibly impressed. Walters half sang and laughed: '*This is the hand, that's shaken the hand, that's shaken the hand of the Führer.*'

Towards the end of the evening I asked Gaisford and Walters if they'd join. They said no. Gaisford said that Mosley was a stuffed shirt and he thought it was a laugh when all the members stood up and toasted the Queen. 'That old bag,' he said. 'I wouldn't cross the road for her. And you told us it was a revolutionary movement that would sweep away the old men from the old parties. Fuck me!

They're like a collection of berks from the local council getting pissed with the mayor.' Walters said the beer wasn't up to much, and Lawson said he admired Mosley's ability to come up with good ideas but thought he was acting all the time. 'He looks like Errol Flynn playing Robin Hood.'

After the rector's marriage to Mrs Simpson we'd moved from Christ Church to St Mark's Church, which was on the wealthier side of Marylebone Road. Outside St Mark's during the build-up to Christmas there was always a large notice showing a number of cars driving towards a small house with a light shining from the top floor. Underneath were the words: 'Wise men worshipped Jesus – they still do.' We were introduced to Father John Crisp, the vicar, and the curate, Father Price. The congregation referred to them as 'Price Crispies'.

Father Crisp was a leading Anglican supporter of the Campaign for Nuclear Disarmament but he also had a wide range of acquaintances. He was a friend of Tom Driberg, the Labour MP, and Jack Spot, the former East End gangster who lived in a flat opposite St Mark's.

When, in his sermons, he attacked the Nazis for committing genocide against the Jews, my mother gathered up our hymn and prayer books, replaced them neatly at the front entrance to the church, and walked home, followed by me. At St Mark's no heads turned, no church warden ran after her to find out if someone was ill, no one cared about such a sudden departure. The indifference disturbed her terribly.

A church warden at St Mark's, when he heard I might still be interested in becoming a clergyman, told me in strict confidence that Father Spencer had spoken to his bishop about the problems with the Grundy family. He'd told the bishop that my mother was a good woman and a 'natural Christian' despite what she said about the Jews. The bishop had suggested that rather than lose a Christian family, St Mark's should contact Mrs Grundy and try to persuade her to change to another church in the area. Hence, the arrival of Father Crisp in our lives.

My mother aged fifteen, around the time she met Mr Lawes.

In my choir robes. My mother hoped I'd become 'the Mosley of the Anglican Church'.

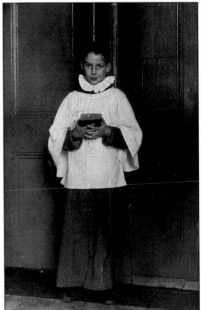

My mother's parents outside their council house in Whitley Bay. As a child, it seemed to me that they wore dark clothes, lived in a dark house and spoke little. It was much more fun visiting my father's parents.

My parents with Grandpa and Grandma Grundy (with me peeping out from behind the bushes). My father was obviously happy to be at Seaton Sluice, but my mother looks rather tense.

Any communication on the subject of this letter should be addressed to:—
THE UNDER SECRETARY
OF STATE,
HOME OFFICE,
LONDON, S.W.1
and the following number quoted:—
862789/2.
Your Ref.

G.2 Division,

HOME OFFICE,

WHITEHALL

16th September, 1944.

Sir,

I am directed by the Secretary of State to inform you that the Restriction Order made against you under Regulation 18A of the Defence (General) Regulations, 1939, has now been revoked.

I am, Sir,
Your obedient Servant,

S. Grundy, Esq.,
66, Loudoun Road,
N.W.8.

The letter announcing the release of my father from prison. 'Only a civil servant could lock you up for four years and sign himself, Your obedient servant,' my mother commented.

Above: Oswald Mosley with his supporters. In the Grundy family, this was a picture to be adored.

My grandest moment in the Movement: aged seventeen, speaking at Trafalgar Square.

Speaking to supporters at Paddington on a Saturday morning, my face intense and strained. (The large neck and head in the foreground belong to my father.)

My other 'leisure activity' – playing the guitar (of sorts) with the Harlequins. (I'm on the far left.)

My mother. I thought that she was magnificent, beautiful, a goddess, a totally indestructible person.

My father in his black shirt. 'I only got involved with Mosley because of your mum,' he said.

My sister Lovene at the coast. Nearly everyone in Union Movement under the age of thirty fell in love with her.

Looking moodily at the Seine in Paris in 1958. My first inklings of what life might be like without the Movement.

Lovene and my mother taking me to the airport to catch a plane to Zambia. Four years passed before I went back to England. This was the last time I was with my mother.

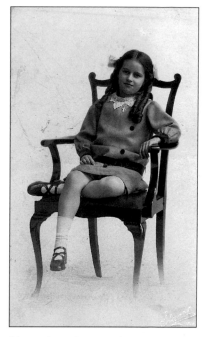

My wary, unhappy mother, shortly before she died.

My mother, photographed in a studio, as a child. In this picture she wears a cross. Like me, she lived a double life, at home she was one thing and to the outside world another. She made my life difficult and complicated but she loved me and I loved her.

Father Crisp took no nonsense from my mother when he came to tea. And he was less than interested in her appeal as a woman. He would wrap his thick blanket-like cape around his shoulders, half hide his face in it and stare at her. The first time he came round he almost dropped his cup when he looked up at the mantelpiece and saw Mosley in his black shirt.

'Mrs Grundy, the leopard doesn't change his spots.'

'Mosley doesn't have to change his spots because he hasn't got any,' replied my mother.

'Therefore, Mrs Grundy, I would assume that your dear Leader was never a leopard. What good news. The way he is presenting himself at the moment he certainly doesn't give the impression of having been a leopard, a lion, or anything at all. Was he always so reasonable, I ask myself?' He pouted at The Leader and turned to Lovene. 'Why can't *I* be your leader?' he asked.

She laughed and said he would look strange in a fencing jacket.

'Because you'd lead in the wrong direction,' interjected my mother.

'Mrs Grundy, if anyone is leading you in the wrong direction it's *that* man.'

The phrase 'that man' was fighting talk in our house.

'What kind of man is he, Mrs Grundy, what kind of man? Mrs Grundy, all I'm asking is that you follow Our Lord and take his words seriously. Our Lord said, "Love thy neighbour as thyself." And St Paul looked to the day when there would be no Jew and no gentile, no man and no woman, just brothers and sisters in Christ. I don't think that I would lead you in the wrong direction. I leave that to the gentleman in the fencing outfit on your mantelpiece.'

I awaited a Mosley-style reply to this outburst but there was only silence. There was no vitriolic counter-attack. My mother said nothing. Regret and sadness clouded her face.

'Lovene,' I heard Father Crisp say as he left the house, 'what are you doing in this strange family? You're its only really intelligent member and you're far too sensitive to be mixed up with this awful movement.' He added, perspicaciously, 'Your mother is going to be a tragic woman. She has Mosley muddled up with Jesus and one day she might see through her wonderful Leader and her whole world will collapse. You and Trevor can get away, but she never will. Confusing an ordinary man with Our Lord is a terrible sin.'

After this confrontation my mother's moods began to swing from intense, almost frenzied, joy to moments of despair. She once grabbed me in the corridor before I left for school and said with utter desperation in her voice, 'Look at me! Look at me! I've been a clown all my life. My God, what's going to happen?'

As a young boy I had dreaded going home, my first question always, 'Has there been a row?' Now, in the middle of my adolescence, I would open the front door, go along to the small kitchen, which my mother increasingly used as a retreat or bunker, open the door and look at her face to see if she was up or down.

'Are you all right, Mum?'

'Of course I'm all right.' And then something like, 'Father Crisp telephoned and said that he'd like you and Lovene to . . . '

At other times she would refuse to speak, and turn away from me into a world of silence, not for hours but sometimes for days.

'It's all to do with something called the change of life,' explained my father, who was immersed in his world of London street maps. 'She'll come out of it. Your mother has never been able to do anything by halves.'

When she was 'on form' my mother used to urge Father Crisp to attend a Mosley meeting. Did she seriously think he would be converted?

'Nicodemus went to hear Jesus,' she said in the kitchen. My father cringed.

At Kensington Town Hall in the middle of that year I noticed Father Crisp sit down in one of the back-row seats. He wore a collar and tie, a suit and a black overcoat, and he looked like a successful businessman. He had responded to my mother's challenge.

After an inspiring performance on the stage which earned Mosley a thunderous round of applause from a cross-section of middle-class South Kensington, there was a question and answer session. A tall, rather striking man in his fifties in an expensive brown leather coat, stood up and addressed a question to Mosley in German. Mosley replied, having learnt that language in prison, and for the next twenty minutes Sir Oswald exchanged ideas on economics and philosophy with the unknown man in a language few people in England could, or wanted to, understand. The audience was stunned and bemused.

Father Crisp, along with dozens of other people, stood up and walked out of the hall, probably grateful that no threatening Blackshirts were waiting to pounce on them for insulting The Leader by leaving early. But the bad old days of the 1930s had gone and Mosley seemed unaware, or indifferent, to the fact that his rather large audience had melted away while he discussed Goethe, Nietzsche and the European Idea with the man in the leather coat. I had learned enough of that language to read parts of *Mein Kampf* in the original, so understood a bit about what the two men were discussing.

Father Crisp spied me standing at one of the exits with a bundle of *Union* newspapers, in which my first contribution to journalism was printed. It was an article calling for the release of Rudolf Hess from Spandau Prison. He knew that I should be at home studying for my A levels. He looked at me and shook his head.

At the end of the meeting, Mosley thanked his stewards and praised them for helping him to mount a very successful campaign. He told us that the slump was on its way and the British people would soon turn to him for leadership.

'Before 1939,' Mosley said, 'even Churchill was seen by the Establishment as a monster, a man with six eyes, eight arms and twelve legs. But when the crisis came, the strongest of Churchill's critics looked around and said, "Who will save us now that war is here? We need a man with six eyes, eight arms . . ."' We laughed and Mosley pushed out his jaw and sunk his hands into the deep pockets of his old grey suit, which had a large silver flash and circle on the left lapel. He flashed his eyes at us and probably made everyone love him just a little bit more. He sent us away that night with dreams in our hearts, knowing that he was right, that no force on earth could stop us.

I looked around for my embryonic youth movement supporters: Les Smith, an ex-public schoolboy; Derek Ashton from Wales, who had, at the last count, thirty-six pictures of Adolf Hitler on his bedroom wall in the small terraced house where he lived close to the Tate Gallery; Gordon Lawson, the tall, handsome young Tenisonian who so closely resembled Hess; three other boys my own age whose parents were Old Members and who had been ordered to take an interest in a new youth movement; and David Bell, from a council flat near Brixton Underground Station. He had heard Mosley speak and had contacted headquarters, which had put him on to me. I later found out that he had been asked to join by the police to find out if a Mosley youth movement was serious or whether it was just another lunatic fringe group which would die a natural death.

I walked out of the hall and across the road to a pub with Les, Gordon and Derek, where we exchanged notes about the enormous victory gained that night and how it would be only a matter of years before The Leader swept to power.

Having talked to Movement secretary, Alf Flockhart, and to Jeffrey Hamm, I told the small group of youth wing supporters, who were starting to worry about the last Tube home, that our first meeting would be held the following week at my house. Everyone should bring a friend and girls would be welcome if they were interested in politics. My father and mother had agreed to let us have the old dark-room in the basement as our permanent headquarters, provided no one smoked.

A few days later, as I prepared to take on leadership of the nation's youth, having shelved plans to become the Mosley of the Anglican Church, the radio was blaring out at Les Smith's house near Paddington. One of his sisters had turned up the BBC in order to hear the words of a new record. It had just leapt into the pop charts, a record everyone was playing, the words of which hardly anyone in Britain understood. It was called 'Heartbreak Hotel'.

I recall making a mental note to say in my opening speech the following week: 'We, the youth of Britain, have finer, more noble things in our lives than rock and roll.'

I asked Les if he would ask his sister to turn down the noise. 'If we're going to have to compete against this bloke Elvis Presley, we'll need really powerful loudspeakers.'

The dark-room was packed. Eighteen people huddled together and, I thought, gave the room a warm and wonderful intimacy. I had invited over thirty people, but eighteen was a good turnout. Hitler had spoken to even smaller gatherings at the beginning, and Mosley had formed the British Union of Fascists with only thirty-two followers, so eighteen wasn't bad.

I started to speak and surprisingly wasn't nervous. 'We have something finer in our lives than rock and roll. I think that most of the people in this room tonight have heard about the greatest living Englishman, Sir Oswald Mosley.'

Les lit up a cigarette, which was out of bounds, but I didn't want to interrupt myself.

'We are privileged to be the junior or younger wing of Union Movement, and I believe that if we take orders from the older people in UM, I mean if we co-operate with them, then we will be able to work miracles for Mosley.

'He has already said that the slump is on its way, and if you saw how he packed them in at Kensington Town Hall, Birmingham, Manchester and other places, you'd understand how close we must be to power.

'We'll start with a sales drive next week at Earl's Court to try and boost the sales of *Union*, and then I think we'll start our own newspaper. I'd like it to be called *Attack*, but the name hasn't been settled. It would be up to a committee of the new youth league to decide. It has been suggested that we start street meetings, and unless anyone objects, I have been asked to address the first one at Praed Street in Paddington on Saturday afternoon at three o'clock, so I hope you'll come along and give us the support we need.'

I thrust my hands into my pockets like Mosley and tried to push out my jaw, but that hurt one of the spots that was developing on my right cheek.

'I think this meeting marks the beginning of something big. I think that we have the spirit to keep us together from now onwards. You know, we don't need a uniform, although that would've been good because it would help us have a kindred spirit, and if ever we do battle with the Reds, a uniform would be of great assistance.'

One of the girls from a school near Tenison's started to shuffle, and said something to Gordon, who had brought her along, and I noticed him look at his watch.

'So, without keeping you any longer, I would like to say that the most important thing in the world right now is to stick with the man who is best for Britain, Oswald Mosley. At the moment, he might appear as a man with six eyes and eight arms, but when the time comes, people choose strong men to lead them. They did that when war broke out, and they took on Winston Churchill and made him an effective dictator of Britain. We have our own man with six eyes and eight arms, Oswald Mosley, and tonight I ask you to support him and if needs be, die for him.'

My mother had supplied tea, in cups borrowed from the Campaign for Nuclear Disarmament branch at St Mark's.

The girl with Gordon left the moment I stopped speaking. She had written me a note and given it to Gordon to pass on to me when he came back to the house after escorting her to the bus stop.

I agreed to come along because you publicised it as a 'Youth for Europe' meeting. I think you should be more honest and tell people your real intentions, and not encourage them to waste money on buses coming from the other side of London to get involved with Fascism, which is evil. How on earth can you be involved in something that supported Hitler? You're far too young to know what you pretend to be talking about. I don't think you know anything about politics or economics or even religion, which you talk about so glibly. I suggest you study hard, get your A levels (if you can) and go to university and learn a bit of modesty.

'Good riddance to bad rubbish,' said Les.

I walked with Gordon to the bus stop in Baker Street, and he told me that his mother was complaining bitterly about his involvement with the Mosley Movement. 'They say it's evil and that Mosley supported Hitler for killing six million Jews.'

'Rubbish,' I said. 'Mosley never supported that, and anyhow the figures are all made up. The Zionists want us to believe Hitler was a monster to justify what they did to the Arabs in Palestine.'

Gordon looked withdrawn and I could tell I was saying goodbye to him.

'Trev, what that girl wrote, read it again. There might be something in it, you know.' And he added, 'When I took her to the bus stop she asked me if you were for real, or if you were being made to say what you said tonight. I think she's right. We're all too young for this. We weren't in the war, and why should we be fighting battles Oswald Mosley fought when he was a Fascist twenty years ago? Why?'

On the way back to Blandford Square I felt sad. I heard 'Heartbreak Hotel' blaring out from a pub in Dorset Square and the music followed me home.

6

The end of 1956 saw something to celebrate in the Grundy household. My sister had become engaged to Bob Row, the editor of *Union*. He was more than twenty years older than Lovene but my mother had encouraged the match, partly because she relished the idea of her daughter marrying into the hierarchy of Union Movement, and partly because it would put pressure on John Wood, who was still devoted to Mosley and in love with Lovene. My mother wanted Lovene to get married and didn't particularly mind if it was to Bob or to John. But John did not have two beans in his pocket at the time and felt in no position to embark on a marriage.

John had first fallen in love with Lovene when he'd seen her presenting flowers to Lady Mosley at a Movement meeting. His mother and father had been Mosley supporters before the war. I can remember his mother well because she looked like the famous character actress Margaret Rutherford. His father was an accountant. They were country members who would have felt quite at home with pro-Mosley author of *Tarka the Otter*, Henry Williamson. The adverse publicity Mosley received for his anti-Jewish remarks embarrassed them and Mrs Wood once told my mother that she was sure it was all nonsense. 'When Sir Oswald comes to talk to us in Wiltshire he never even mentions the Jews,' she said. 'He talks about farming and very sensibly too, I might add.'

Lovene's and Bob's engagement was officially announced at the major annual Movement dinner and afterwards I heard my mother say to my sister, who appeared almost distraught, 'Well, if Johnny wants you he'll do something about it, won't he?'

Lovene rarely wore her engagement ring and though she was only twenty-one she developed a sad, withdrawn look, which may well have increased her appeal to the two men caught up in my mother's Machiavellian game.

After Christmas lunch, Bob and I went for a walk in Regent's Park. The lake was frozen over and we had taken bread for the ducks, but I had eaten most of it by the time we reached the black rim of the sheet of water. This lake was my childhood and early manhood retreat, my place of exile, my second home and my only experience of the transitory beauty of nature.

'When Mosley comes to power,' said Bob, who was striding out like the countryman he was, 'boys like you will be groomed for leadership. You know, Trevor, the English system stinks and it must go. The Leader is in full agreement and once told me the worst time of his life was at prep school and Winchester. He said the best time of his life was in the trenches during the First World War with ordinary men from all walks of life. He told Jeffrey Hamm that when he broke with the old political parties and formed the BUF he wanted to put men back into uniform to re-create the camaraderie, because it was the only time he had seen men all pulling together for a common purpose, without class divisions.'

After Mosley, Bob Row was my biggest hero, a man far more important to me than Elvis Presley, or the crop of rock singers who were sprouting up in Britain as 1957 approached.

Bob had two weeks' holiday a year and walked alone in the Lake District, where he came from. He smoked thirty cigarettes a day while he was there, but gave up the habit the moment he returned to his shared *Union* editor's office at 302 Vauxhall Bridge Road. He would also give up normal food during his break and go on a strict diet of brown bread and molasses. He laughed when he asked me if I had ever seen a Jew eating white bread. 'They know that all the nutrition has been taken out of white bread and that's why it's good enough for the gentiles or the *goyim,* as they call us.' I soon stopped eating white bread.

Bob earned a pittance and couldn't afford to get married, but Mosley might pay him more now, although, he explained, without even a hint of criticism, Mosley was scraping the bottom of the financial barrel in France to pay for next year's campaign in Britain. The Old Man also had to keep travelling and meeting people on the Continent in order to explain European problems to his followers that side of the Channel. So, there wouldn't be spare cash for higher salaries just because the editor of *Union* wanted to indulge in the luxury of marriage.

'Always remember how Hitler and the National Socialists suffered before they came to power,' he told me. 'But there's another, brighter, side to look forward to. Things'll be vastly different when The Leader comes to power. I'll be one of the highest paid journalists in the country, probably running *The Times* or the *Daily Telegraph* or a new Union Movement paper. And you'll have a job under me to begin with, and one day might even . . .'

We went on like this hour after hour, living in a world of fairy-tale fantasy, anticipating what would happen to us all when Mosley came to power.

Bob told me that The Leader was preparing for a new pre-war style political offensive in Britain.

'Why is the Leader so convinced that now is the right time?' I asked.

'The Commies want to disarm Britain so that the Reds can march into Europe from Berlin. OM is writing about it in next month's *European*. You know, you should start writing for the *European*.'

Bob said that The Leader had been told about my work with the youth league and would like to meet me when he came across to London in January. 'The Leader is particularly impressed with what Jeffrey Hamm has told him about your street meetings. Mosley said that he's quite prepared to meet you and other Movement speakers to give you some hints.'

The following week, I told Les and Derek and some of the other boys who were hanging around youth headquarters at Blandford Square that when Mosley came to power we would be part of a new élite. The public schools would be taken over by the Movement and we would be enrolled, along with thousands of other boys, so we could learn the ideas of Mosley's new age of Europe a Nation – Africa the Empire. We would be encouraged to do national service in Rhodesia and South Africa to help strengthen white rule and, at the same time, make life better for the blacks who were at a completely different stage of development from us.

By the time I was seventeen years of age I had spoken all over London for the youth league.

'Be careful that you don't burn yourself out before you're eighteen,' said one old-timer who had supported Mosley since the formation of the BUF, a quarter of a century earlier. 'I've seen young men like you before give everything to Mosley. They burn them-selves out and you never hear of them again.'

Was this old-timer for or against Mosley, I asked Don Lucas, who was in his late thirties. A blond-haired Hitler fanatic, he lived in a flat near Hammersmith Bridge with his mother and an Alsatian dog called Blondi. At meetings he wore a white shirt, a black tie with a Movement pin stuck in it, black trousers and shiny shoes. His prize possession was a black leather belt with a silver flash and circle buckle.

'That old codger,' replied Don. 'He once told me that a million people had been through the BUF in the 1930s, but that most stayed only a few weeks. They joined after hearing the Old Man and left as soon as they found out nothing happened afterwards. I wish we had a few of that million now.'

Don had been ordered not to wear his belt because Mosley had banned uniforms along with the Fascist salute, but it did not dampen his enthusiasm. Every Saturday he would stand on a flimsy wooden platform in Praed Street, throw out his arms and his growing stomach, and ask a handful of listeners what had happened to the greatest Empire the world had ever known. 'Where are the men who went out in little ships to unknown places to build a civilisation, the likes of which has not been seen since the days of Rome?'

An Irish drunk at the nearby Scotch Ale House shouted back, 'They're all in here, ya silly sod.'

At the end of Paddington meetings we would sell a few copies of *Union*, but soon would head for a Movement-friendly pub. Youth league supporters were all under age, but no one in the pub minded.

Derek was becoming increasingly unbalanced and told me that he was a reincarnation of Horst Wessel, the Nazi martyr. The most recent tally revealed that Derek now had forty-two pictures of Hitler on his bedroom wall and it made me nervous to discover that among them he had stuck up one of me.

The handful of Tenison's boys I'd managed to interest in the Movement mostly lasted as long in the youth league as Gordon Lawson who, since that night at the bus stop in Baker Street, had left the sixth form and gone to live in northern Germany. He said he wanted to become a writer and learn German.

Possible school recruits were protected from Union Movement by angry parents who had fought against Hitler and Mussolini. One boy I had tried to recruit in the lower fifth form had been cross-examined by members of the Labour Party in Streatham. One of his inquisitors had written to Dr Robinson about my extramural activities. The name Grundy started to stink at Archbishop Tenison's, but this time the headmaster did not call me to his study.

However, early one afternoon in a music class I laughed aloud at something a fellow pupil had said concerning Beethoven's deafness. Mr Burton, whose favourite I had been in the days when I'd wanted to be a clergyman, abruptly turned the music off.

He fixed me with his gaze as if he were trying to annihilate me with his glare, then pulled me towards him by the ear as if I was a small child. I pushed his hand aside. 'I am seventeen,' I thought, 'leader of Mosley Youth and not some backstreet urchin.'

'You're a rotten apple, Grundy. You're a boy who has been given every opportunity and you have thrown them all away, one by one. If you weren't a sixth-former, I would cane you. You are an insult to the name of the school. Get out of this class and don't ever come back.'

I returned to my desk, picked up my books, took my bicycle clips out of my locker and rode towards Vauxhall Bridge. I chained the bicycle to the railings at 302 Vauxhall Bridge Road and went up the stairs to see Bob Row.

'Bob, I can't take school any more,' I said. 'I want to leave. Can't you get me a job here? I'll do anything. I know The Leader hasn't got any money but it's known I'm Movement at school and they're starting to make my life hell on earth. They're bastards, real bastards.'

Bob looked weary. He completed a headline. 'Mosley warned the West,' it read. It hung over an article of about three thousand words written by a special correspondent in Newcastle, almost certainly Bob Row because there was no money to pay anyone else.

We went next door to the Café Europa for a cup of tea. Bob bought me a cake and told me to cheer up. He said he would find out from Jeffrey Hamm whether they could take me on at 302, but was I really ready to leave school and work full-time for the Movement? I would only get a few pounds a week, at the most four.

I told him, 'Yes, definitely yes.' I would study in the evenings for my A levels, pass them and still go on to university, or a teachers' training college, or whatever. Bob looked at me and smiled, but his eyes were sad.

'Do you know about Lovene?' he asked. 'She's broken off our engagement and is going to marry Johnnie Wood. I'll kill him,' said Bob. 'Everything has been destroyed. Everything. My whole life, all my hopes.'

I loved Bob, as a much older brother, a father-figure and role model. I stayed with him in his office all afternoon and when it came time to go home I rang my mother and told her I was with Bob Row and was helping him with *Union*, always an acceptable excuse.

Some time after nine o'clock I rode home through Hyde Park, asking myself why life was so complicated. Why did Lovene love John more than Bob? Why had Mr Burton suddenly blown his top at me? And why were people who condemned Mosley for being intolerant so intolerant themselves?

Lovene's wedding took place at St Mark's Church and I was best man in my Archbishop Tenison's blazer. We stood together for a group photograph: Lovene and John, my father and mother, myself and, a few paces away, looking on, Father Crisp. We look as happy as if this was our last minute on earth before being escorted by the priest to a bullet-scarred wall to be shot.

Afterwards, Lovene and John cut the cake, which he had bought that morning. We all drank some wine and Lovene played the Mario Lanza record I had bought her for her eighteenth birthday. We all adored Mario because when he was young he had recorded the 'Giovenezza' for Mussolini.

Shortly before Easter I received a telephone call from Jeffrey Hamm. He wanted me to go from school to headquarters that afternoon to hear something of great importance. I was certain that I had got the job with Union Movement.

I was hopelessly behind with my A level schoolwork in history, English literature and geography. Much of my time in the sixth form was free time but I spent it writing articles for *Union* or at Marylebone Public Library, trying to read books, which I couldn't understand, about Wagner and Shaw, Spengler's *Decline of the West* and the sensation of 1957, Colin Wilson's *The Outsider*. Rumours were rife throughout the Movement that the real author of *The Outsider* was Mosley. He had, the rumours claimed, let Colin Wilson take the credit, the glory and the money but they were all Mosley's ideas.

At four o'clock I rushed from school to 302 and stood in the bookshop waiting to be called.

'Come up, Trevor.' It was Jeffrey Hamm's unmistakable voice. I sat down opposite him; it felt like being called in to the headmaster.

Jeffrey Hamm had taken over as the Movement's secretary following the imprisonment of Alf Flockhart, who had been convicted of 'interfering' with a man in a public lavatory. My mother said that he had been framed by the Jews, but it was his second conviction. After he went to jail, stories circulated about Wednesday-night activities in the basement of 302, when some of the members practised the drums in preparation for the return of the good old days of Mosley street campaigns throughout Britain. The office workers at 302 jokingly referred to the Drum Corps as the Bum Corps, but the conviction was taken very seriously by East End members who informed Mosley in a letter that if Flockhart was ever seen again at headquarters, or allowed to rejoin the Movement, they would all resign.

Jeffrey Hamm said, 'I haven't spoken to The Leader about you joining us on a full-time basis and, quite honestly, I don't think it's a good idea because you're so close to taking your A levels. Why throw away an opportunity of going to university? Mosley needs people in the universities. I know your life is being made a misery at school but try and stick it out.

'But there is some good news.' He smiled broadly. 'At least, I hope you will see it that way. OM will not be speaking at Trafalgar Square this year. He's tied up with a series of extremely important meetings in Venice. So I have taken a decision which will surprise a lot of people.' He paused for effect. 'I will be the main speaker at this year's rally and that meeting will be opened, I hope, by a certain young man who has made an indelible impression on us all. That young man is you. This year's Trafalgar Square rally will be opened by you, followed by me as the Movement's most senior speaker after The Leader. I offer you my congratulations for your wonderful per-formances and speeches all over London.'

I went home in a dream. I had left all my homework at 302 in a briefcase but didn't care if I never saw Chaucer's *Canterbury Tales* or Wedgwood's *Thirty Years War* again.

I got off the train at Baker Street and walked past the café in Regent's Park where as a boy I had eaten biscuits and drunk orange juice with Timothy, past the pitches where I had kicked footballs, hit cricket balls, read books and spied shyly on girls in their green and grey uniforms.

'And now I am a man,' I said aloud to one of the swans on the lake.

It looked at me. Was it really a swan or was it Parsifal, the swan knight in disguise, offering me his congratulations? Parsifal, who Mosley said represented the highest form of spiritual development in man's onward and upward journey.

I continued walking around the Inner Circle, through Queen Mary's Gardens, down past Madame Tussauds and past Marylebone Library, where almost every night I put at least one hand-sized sticker on the public notice board. 'Support Mosley: Europe a Nation – Africa the Empire.'

In just two weeks' time I would stand on the plinth at the base of Nelson's Column in Trafalgar Square and everyone in the world whom I loved and admired would be there, loving and admiring me. And I would speak from my heart and soul.

That night I stared deep into the steamy bathroom mirror. 'My friends, our task is hard but I ask you this afternoon here in Trafalgar Square, at Easter 1957, to sacrifice your all so that Britain can be great again.'

When I told my mother, she was delighted and said that on the big day some of her make-up could be used to help disguise the spots which had started to appear in alarming numbers on my increasingly gaunt face.

So, like some teenage vicar, I retreated to my room to prepare my speech or sermon. My mother, melodramatic as usual, said that I should speak as if it was the last time before I died. This had to be a great memorial to Mosley, she said.

I now had Lovene's old room. Since her marriage to John she had taken over the basement and transformed it into an arty den, full of bright pictures, curtains, carpets, wall-hangings and music by Tchaikovsky, Chopin and Debussy, who were being popularised by long-playing records.

In my new room, sandwiched between the front room and the kitchen, where my mother spent most of her time, was a large framed picture of Mosley in a black fencing-type shirt, signed by him in white chalk or crayon. Over my bed there were cut-outs from magazines of Brigitte Bardot, Marilyn Monroe and Anthony Perkins, who had replaced Tony Curtis as the person I most wanted to resemble.

Between my room and the kitchen was a cubby-hole of a lavatory. Every grunt could be heard. When summer came and the windows were wide open it was sometimes embarrassing inviting people to my room to talk about politics. I would pray that no one would use the lavatory while I was telling potential recruits about Mosley.

I played records to them of The Leader speaking in the 1930s and used to explain how Wagner, through his music, especially *Götter-dämmerung*, had shown that the old order was doomed. The new order would be an age of science and discovery, peace and harmony, brought about by the emergence of a man who was beyond Sigmund, and even beyond Siegfried, a man as indifferent to power as he was to personal wealth because he already had both and didn't need the gold which corrupted all honest politicians. I didn't have a clue what I was talking about but I was able to repeat much that I had heard from the lips of Bob Row when he had courted Lovene in this same room, with me, his attentive pupil, sitting close to his feet.

Mosley had told Bob that when he planned a speech he kept in mind Wagner's operas. He said he felt Wagner in his soul when he was speaking and always tried to build up to a climax which would bring even his fiercest critics to their feet. When that happened, he said, the experience was unforgettable and dangerously addictive.

During the days before Trafalgar Square I studied not for my A levels but to perfect my speech, which I had to memorise, because no Union Movement speaker ever used notes. I would make it general and beat the drum only on subjects I had heard Mosley talk about: the decline of British power; the loss of the Empire during an unnecessary war against Germany; and the fact that Britain's leadership still hesitated to work towards unity with Europe, which alone could make Britain independent of the big powers, America and the Soviet Union.

In the New Europe there would be not only a common market but a common government for a people who shared four thousand years of history. Africa would be Europe's new Empire and would provide

Europeans with every mineral they required and enough space to absorb all their unemployed.

Eventually, I would say, Europeans will have the highest standard of living in the world. Then Communism will collapse because they can see for themselves just how well Europe is doing under Mosley's system.

I would also touch on the lack of meaning and commitment in modern Britain. How young people were now being asked to keep away from serious political organisations such as Union Movement. I took as my theme what Jimmy Porter said in John Osborne's play *Look Back in Anger*. In a moment of despair, Porter cried out that all the good, brave causes had been fought in the 1930s and that if the 'big bang' came and everyone died in a nuclear war it would be about as pointless, meaningless and inglorious as stepping in front of a bus. I wrote down beside that quote in the book: 'Yes, without Mosley it would be like this.' Then I wrote, 'But there are great, brave causes left and the building of Europe and Africa is one of them. What glory then!'

For most of the weekend, I lay by the lake in Regent's Park scribbling notes, tearing them up, and starting again. It had to be perfect and it could only be ten minutes long.

On the morning of the day, my mother was in a state of nerves. 'No one disturb Trevor,' she said in a loud voice as she brought me in a cup of tea, two boiled eggs and some bread and butter cut up into soldiers.

I didn't stay at home for lunch. Les called round and we walked down to Marylebone Underground Station. I was wearing a white shirt, black tie and trousers and an old school mackintosh. Les said that he would stand behind me on the plinth with a flag.

Jeffrey Hamm arrived at Trafalgar Square with Bob Row and others from headquarters in a large van known as 'The Elephant'. It had carried The Leader around London and across Britain, and had iron bars over the windows. Bob shook my hand and Jeffrey asked if I was all right, and would I keep the speech to ten minutes.

Initially, there were only a couple of hundred people in the square but by ten minutes to three the numbers had swollen to several thousand. There was a noisy group from the Young Communist League and a group of students carrying 'Down with South Africa' banners. One scruffy youth had a banner which read 'Don't blow up the world' and although there were quite a few policemen in the vicinity there were also many tourists, photographers and pigeons.

Our flag-bearers used a wooden box to climb onto the plinth at the foot of Nelson's famous column and walked across to stand behind me.

At three o'clock, I took off my mackintosh, stuck a flash and circle pin in my tie and approached the microphone. The sequence was filmed in black and white without any sound and when I later saw it, it reminded me of a Charlie Chaplin film. I noticed that I looked nervous and walked with a stoop.

Before the speech, one Old Member had advised me to concentrate on just one person in the crowd, or to pretend I was speaking to cabbages.

I started the usual way, welcoming friends to a great meeting in London, which showed that no power on earth could stifle the truth.

There was loud jeering and booing and some laughter from the Communist part of the crowd. I took no notice and concentrated on the top of the microphone. Hamm had said, 'Take no notice unless they throw something. Then we'll step in and deal with them.'

I said that the youth of Europe were waiting for the youth of Britain to lead them into a bright new age, an age without Communism, without exploitation, an age with a future. 'Last year, students in Hungary defied the entire might of the Russian war machine. Young men and women picked up stones from the streets of Budapest and hurled them against tanks and guns and those tanks and guns roared back the Communist answer to freedom. Students were shot like dogs and that was at a time when our own government, the government led by Eden, saw fit to co-operate with Israel and France and attack Egypt. That, my friends, gave Khrushchev the excuse to go in. He said, "Well, if Eden can back the forces of oppression, so can I, and there'll be no one around with the moral right to condemn me." It was

117

the *great betrayal* and one day our government will stand before the bar of history and be condemned, utterly condemned.'

I put my hands on my hips like Mosley. 'Some people say that there are no great, brave, noble causes left. But how wrong can they be? No great causes? What about the cause of freeing the youth of Europe from the oppression of Communism and Russian tanks? Isn't that a great and noble cause? And if we died for that, would it be as pointless, as meaningless, as "stepping under a bus", as John Osborne said in his play *Look Back in Anger*?' I leant forward, imitating The Leader. 'Look forward with hope! That's what we say in Union Movement. Not look back in anger but look forward in hope!'

I heard jeers and then a very loud voice shouted, 'Piss off!'

I looked in the heckler's direction. 'We know where help won't be coming from!' Our side cheered. I saw the Grundy contingent standing by one of the fountains. My mother's eyes bored into me. Nearby were James and several of the other people who'd been my extended family since I was ten years old. James smiled and gave me a thumbs-up sign.

'Oswald Mosley, more than any other politician in Britain, understands young people. After the First World War he returned to England and found the old men sitting in the same soft leather chairs they'd sat in before Europe went to war in 1914. In those chairs were the men who'd made millions while the youth of Europe tore each other to pieces. And the get-rich-quick gang still runs Britain. They dared call Mosley a traitor in 1940 when he said that if we went to war against Germany we'd lose everything we'd ever fought for – the Empire. Mosley, a traitor? Mosley, the man who served in the trenches in France? Mosley, who nearly lost his leg? Mosley, who served with the Royal Flying Corps? Mosley, who crashed and was nearly killed and even today walks with a limp? And those fat old men in their soft leather chairs dared call him a traitor!'

A man shouted, 'Pity he survived!'

I said he was the youngest MP since Pitt and heard, 'Pitt the shit!' and then, 'What do you know about the First World War, you spotty-faced git?'

I looked down towards the voice and said, 'The youth of Britain are with Mosley. Happily for all of us, that doesn't include you.'

Applause from our side.

'Mosley wanted to see real change in Britain, a revolution – not that you lot' – I looked at the Communists – 'would know how to spell the word, because you're too busy killing students in Hungary.

'But every change, every hope was thrown away in 1940 when they locked up Mosley and one thousand British patriots who opposed the war. Yet when war was declared, my friends, Hitler was marching *east*, not *west*. We declared war on Germany not in a *British* quarrel but rather in a . . . in a *foreign* quarrel. And had it not been for the scientists who invented the A-bomb the Russians would today be in Trafalgar Square and where would free speech be?'

A man standing with a sheep dog raised his hand and then screamed out, 'Where the hell would free speech be if Hitler and his thugs had won the war?' He put down his hand and walked away, his large dog wagging its tail.

I looked at my watch. A minute to go. One of the Communists held a copy of *Union*. Without taking his eyes off me, he lit the paper with a cigarette lighter, dropped it on the floor and watched the crisp, ragged ball of brown cinders bounce towards one of the policemen standing between me and the crowd. It captured the front row's attention. I stood and watched it burn and then looked up.

'Burn a newspaper. How brave. How courageous. But, my dear friend who has nothing else to do, with no great cause to live for you will never burn or destroy this movement because behind us stand the people of Britain who have not yet spoken, the people who will one day turn to the only man who has never betrayed them, the man once called "traitor" but who will one day be called "hero" – Oswald Mosley, the one man who stands today between the free British people and the forces of International – *In-ter-na-tion-al* – Communism.'

Our lot cheered wildly. The Communists laughed and booed and then crossed the road. A large anti-apartheid demonstration was building up outside South Africa House.

Jeffrey Hamm mounted the plinth and walked towards me with a serious look on his face. My first thought was: Should I have said International *Jewish* Communism instead of just International Communism? But no, he had his hand out and was moving quickly towards me and suddenly it was over, the ordeal was over and he was smiling and I was smiling and I could hear cheers and clapping and could see waving and laughing from our supporters.

'You were wonderful,' Jeffrey said, grasping my hand. 'Wonderful. That showed them. Well done . . . even when they burnt the paper . . . well done.'

For a short time I stood on my own in the crowd and then slightly aside with Les and Derek, who gazed at me. I thought: 'He's going to touch me to gain strength.'

I noticed a tall, good-looking young man staring at me. I tried to guess his age: somewhere between twenty and twenty-five, I thought. He wore a dark blue, expensive-looking overcoat and was tall with brown hair and dark eyes. For one moment I thought I was looking at the young Sir Oswald.

He approached me to shake my hand and said, 'You spoke well. You're a credit to the Movement. I congratulate you.' There was a silver pin in his lapel, which I recognised as the symbol of the Falange Party in Spain.

As he walked away I saw that he was joined by a small man with long grey hair and a lovely blonde girl.

'Who was that?' I asked Freddie Shepherd, a North Islington branch member.

'Don't you know who that was, you silly tart?' Freddie called everyone in the Movement, apart from The Leader, a silly tart. 'That's Alexander Mosley, The Leader and Lady Mosley's eldest son. He's supposed to be a genius like his father. I've never seen him at a meeting before, though he hangs around 302 quite a lot.'

'I'm sure I know the people he's with,' I remarked.

'You should, you silly tart. That's Sid Proud, your brother-in-law's boss and that's Cynthia, his daughter. Can't miss her, can you? Not with those knockers, you can't.'

I walked towards my parents, Lovene and Johnnie.

When Jeffrey Hamm finished his speech about economics, Mosley's wage-price mechanism and the need for a common currency as well as a common government in Europe, he came up to me and shook my hand warmly again.

'Mrs Grundy,' he said, looking at my mother. 'Quite a performance today, eh? We'll make a Mosley speaker of him yet.'

7

Mosley kept his promise and one Saturday afternoon, not long after my Trafalgar Square triumph, I was invited to headquarters to meet him.

I put on my only casual jacket, which I was buying on hire purchase from a shop in Edgware Road with money I earned from Chiltern Stores as chief delivery boy on a Saturday morning, nine shillings for four hours' work and about seven and sixpence in tips. It was a powder blue Johnnie Ray jacket and I wore dark trousers, my usual black shoes, white shirt and blue tie.

I waited in the narrow corridor by the bookshop at 302 until Jeffrey Hamm came out of The Leader's small office and said, 'This way, Grundy', as if I was some promising cadet called in to see the general. I nervously entered the room as Jeffrey Hamm left it and came face to face for the first time with the man my mother had turned into a god, and mixed up, both in her mind and mine, with Jesus Christ.

'Sit down, Grundy,' said The Leader. 'You've been doing good work for the Movement, I hear.'

Mosley had grown quite heavy. He was wearing his familiar grey suit, but there was no large silver flash and circle in his lapel. He looked at me with small, button-like eyes. He's trying to hypnotise me, I thought. Even though I worshipped him, I remember thinking, as Lovene had all those years before, 'You're like a fox, a great big fox.'

'Jeffrey Hamm has told me that you want to expand the youth wing of the Movement,' Mosley said. 'I approve. I want to see you young people forming branches all over Britain. I don't want to see older people, older members, mixed up with the youth,' he added. 'I don't believe anyone over, say, twenty-five should be in the youth movement. Twenty-one. No one in the youth movement over the age of twenty-one, do you agree?'

I agreed, thinking, 'You've said that because of Alf Flockhart and the Bum Corps.'

'May we call the movement Mosley Youth?' I asked.

He smiled. 'I'd find that very flattering. You spoke well at Trafalgar Square, Grundy. I'm glad you weren't fazed when Communists burnt *Union*.' He paused. 'I'll let you into a secret,' he said and leant slightly forward and flashed his eyes. '*Union* will be renamed *Action*.' That was the name of the paper before the war. I wanted to ask him if he was going to bring back the salute but didn't. 'I'm pleased to hear that young speakers never mentioned Jews from the platform, Grundy,' he continued. 'In fact, if we had some Jewish members that would be a good thing.'

Did he wink at me? Perhaps something had got into his right eye. But now he looked quite gentle and concerned and said something that briefly changed the atmosphere created by hero-worshipper meeting hero. He became almost fatherly.

'How are your parents? Good people. And your mother? You're very fond of and close to your mother. I was very close to my mother.' There was a lengthy silence and then he said in military fashion, 'Good. Thank you for coming to see me.'

I had been dismissed.

When I reached home, still exhilarated from the meeting, my mother told me that there was wonderful news. The Leader's son, Alexander, had telephoned and asked to speak to me. 'He sounded just like OM,' said my mother. 'Do you know what he said, Trevor? He said that he had heard a lot about me and that a lot of the people in the East End said that Lady Mosley was the best advertisement for The Leader and that Mrs Grundy was a good second because she was always at meetings and did canvassing and had produced the young man who was going to do so much for the Movement. He sounded just like The Leader. Just like him.'

I returned the call and Alexander didn't sound like The Leader at all. He told me he was with his brother, Max, and did I want to speak to him?

The voice at the other end said, 'Watcha mate. Are you Mosley yufe, like, gonna go and see Bill 'Aley wiv me and me bruvver or are ya goin' out on some sales drive, like?'

Bill Haley had earlier arrived in Britain from the United States and had been thumping out 'Rock Around the Clock'. Teenagers were ripping up seats and girls were wetting themselves at cinema houses all over Britain.

I told Max Mosley that I didn't like Bill Haley, though I thought Elvis had a good voice.

'Well, mate, we'll 'ave to get Elvis then, won't we? If Bill 'Aley ain't no good we'll 'ave to get Elvis and see what 'appens then, like, won't we, mate?' Then he said in his normal voice, 'You know, Trevor, there are five million teenagers in this country with an annual purchasing power of £800 million. Could you tell me, only as a rough estimate, of course, how many have joined your branch of the Youth Movement and what percentage of their income is spent on Union Movement products?'

Alexander said, after a suitable pause for reaction and their laughter, 'I'm sorry about that, Trevor, but my brother has just been on an advanced English course in Limehouse and will be all right after a long lie down.'

I arranged to meet Alexander at an Italian coffee bar which had opened next to the Classic Cinema in Baker Street.

The phone was handed back to Max. 'Sorry, can't make it meself, Trevor, but might see yer next week. Me? Ahm goin' dawn the Two Is coffee bar in Soho, considerin' it's Sa'erday night, like, ter listen ter Tommy Steele or Marty Wilde. Like Marty, I do. Bit like Elvis.'

Max was exactly a month younger than me and I had often said in speeches that when the police came to arrest Lady Mosley in 1940 they had taken her away from her baby, and how terrible that was.

I asked my father if he would lend me ten shillings so I could have coffee with Alexander Mosley. To my surprise, he gave me fifteen shillings and said that if the money was spent on The Leader's son that was all right with him.

I wandered down to Baker Street and stood outside the café. By the cinema there was a lengthy queue of people waiting to see one of the old black-and-white classics. I waited for five minutes, which stretched into ten. I noticed that people in the queue, most of them duffel-coated members of some university or college, identifiable because of their colourful scarves, were becoming a little embarrassed by the presence of a tall hunchback who was limping along the line of cinema-goers with one hand out. When I looked more closely, I realised that the beggar was Alexander Mosley. I was about to spend some time with the son of one of the outrageous Mitford girls who seemed to see life as one big joke.

When Alexander noticed me, he straightened up and smiled. 'Trevor, how nice to see you,' he said in a loud, exaggerated upper-class drawl, as if to say to those in the queue, 'I was only having a bit of fun. I was just joking.'

There were many stares in our direction.

We went into the café for coffees and I had enough money to suggest a couple of spaghetti Bolognaises. Alexander, who was two years older than me and much taller, spoke to the waiter in fluent Italian. He told me that he could also speak French, German, Spanish and Gaelic. He imitated the latter beautifully to the amusement of two pretty young girls at the next table.

'I'm sorry Max was such a pain,' Alexander said. 'It was all a joke, a bit of a giggle. It's just that he finds it hard to believe that a teenage boy living in the middle of London, surrounded by millions of girls his own age, could spend Saturday afternoons on a platform and Saturday evenings selling *Union* newspapers at Underground stations.' It didn't take me long to pick up the message that both Max and Alexander regarded me as odd, perhaps mentally backward. But why had he bothered to ring me up? Why was he showing interest?

Alexander told me that he and Max had been brought up in Ireland and that during the holidays Max had gone off on his own on a pony with food and drink and often hadn't returned home for days. He said that one night the family home had been burnt to the ground. No one ever found out what had started it, but a lot of secret papers had been destroyed. He'd been alone with his father and they'd fought the blaze together and rescued an elderly woman housekeeper.

I told him I knew they had lived in Ireland because our Christmas cards from the Mosley family came either from headquarters or from somewhere in Southern Ireland.

'We send people Christmas cards?' Alexander asked. 'I didn't know that. Who sends them? Not my mother, surely?'

He told me that he didn't want to go to university and he didn't know what he wanted to do with his life, maybe become a barrister, maybe a writer. 'What I'd really like to be is God.'

'I might become a vicar,' I said, trying not to be outdone. Alexander stared at me. I thought he was going to stand up and leave, but then the girls at the next table laughed and he smiled at them and said something in Spanish, which sparked off more giggling. There was guitar music on the juke box and Alexander threw his head back to imitate a matador.

He said that he worked for a travel agency and went to Spain regularly.

'You work for Sid Proud,' I said and told him that my brother-in-law was John Wood, who also worked for Mr Proud.

'Sid Proud works for me,' said Alexander. 'He wants me to marry his daughter and become a partner.'

I asked him if he had many friends in London and he said he hadn't any friends anywhere. 'But now I have met you I will call round to your house, if I may. Your mother said I should, at any time of the day or night, which was kind of her. Your parents are Old Members, aren't they?'

I told him about my father in the war and how my mother had first seen Mosley in Brighton, his hair glistening from the rain. How he had spoken that night, how she worshipped him and thought he alone could save England from doom.

'Oh God,' he said. 'Old Members . . . old ruins,' and he did an impression of a man falling fast asleep.

We left the café and I walked back to Blandford Square, Alexander to his room in Chelsea. I had to get to bed early because Sunday morning was Islington street market, where Mosley Youth usually attracted a crowd of twenty or even thirty people. Unfortunately, most of them were Islington branch members. From there we'd go in one of the older member's cars for an afternoon *Union* sales drive, either at Earl's Court Underground or outside Brompton Oratory, which was Catholic and had a large number of Irish members, who favoured Mosley because he'd spoken out against the Black and Tans in the 1920s.

The Mosley youth league was made up of not much more than a wooden speaker's platform painted shiny black, ten active members and a weekly column in *Union*, which told the readership of about one thousand subscribers and a few hundred people who bought it at Underground stations in London about our activities. I'd write the column and Bob Row gave it prominence so it looked as if we were an important arm of Union Movement. Considering the number of meetings I addressed in a month, we were probably the most active part of the Movement.

Still spinning from Mosley's successful meetings of the previous year, 1957 was a busy year for all of us. Coaches were hired from friends in the East End transport business and sometimes on a Sunday morning we would make for the south coast, or Southend. When Birmingham or Manchester wanted to publicise a meeting or a sales drive, we'd drive up north.

Once we'd arrived, the beer crates would appear from the back of the coach and the drinking and singing would start. The usual slogans would be shouted and then nostalgic BUF songs such as 'Bye Bye Blackshirts', to the tune of 'Bye Bye Blackbird', and the anti-Jewish 'Abie, Abie, Abie my boy, What are you waiting for now?' The latter song was about a Jewish youth, reluctant to marry, facing his future father-in-law. When the word *Abie* was intoned, members would rub their noses and hunch their backs to imitate what they thought was a caricature of a Fagan-type nineteenth-century Jew.

After half a dozen beers each, sleeves were rolled up and sometimes shirts removed to reveal swastika and flash-and-circle tattoos, along with old scars from battles against Jews and Communists. Voices and bottles would be raised as the 'Giovenezza' and Horst Wessel song were belted out, with some old-timers singing the latter in German, while passing cars and coaches were given the Nazi salute to the amazement, and anger, of holiday-makers, boy scouts, girl guides and church groups out for the day to the coast.

I watched my loyal youth league comrade, Les, with increasing despair because I felt a bit responsible for him, even though he was older than me. He had been sent to some minor public school when he was eleven but had been unable to keep up academically. He'd received occasional private tuition but failed his O levels and got a job behind the counter in a clothing shop near Marble Arch. He was later caught taking money from the till and was on probation when he drifted towards the youth league after hearing me speak at Praed Street.

Les had a large and usually half-open mouth, which made him look rather moronic. He had become the effective 'girlfriend' of Freddie Shepherd and they had their arms around one another most of the time in the back seat of the coach. Les suddenly had a great deal of money at his disposal and when he bought drinks in the pub he flashed it around ostentatiously.

He saw me looking at him as he was performing at the bar one night and said aggressively, 'Don't look at me like that, Trevor. Freddie's got the money and gives some of it to me. So what? If you want to carry parcels of food up to Jews in Bickenhall Mansions on a Saturday morning for nine bob, that's up to you. I don't.'

Derek always stood loyally next to the speaker's platform when I was on it and would come along to the bars, too, but he didn't drink alcohol and would usually sit on his own and read a book about economic reform in Hitler's Germany. I noticed in one of his books the script was Gothic. 'Can you understand all that stuff?' I asked him.

'I like the pictures,' he said.

By the time we got back to 302, most of the members were drunk; a few papers had been sold; I'd told Southend, or Bournemouth, about the 'new heaven' and the 'new earth' which would arrive shortly after Mosley was voted into power; Don Lucas had alienated a few hundred people by slapping his rapidly growing stomach, which was almost too big for his BUF belt, and telling passers-by and residents of Southend's pier district that, 'If there hadn't been a war against Hitler, Europe would be ruled by whites, there'd be no Russians or Turks in Germany, France wouldn't be fighting a war against Communist Algerians, Britain wouldn't be fighting Communist Mau Mau murderers in Kenya and there would be no West Indians in Brixton.' He used to end his speeches, 'Keep Brixton White – KBW – Keep Britain White.'

At the end of meetings some of the older men in the crowd would come up to me and say I was a good speaker but should be speaking for the Labour Party.

'But they've betrayed the working class,' I'd say.

One old man said, 'Mosley? Thought he was dead. Should have hanged him with that other fellow, Lord Haw-Haw.'

The week after an outing, my column 'Youth on the March' would tell how a group of dedicated young men and women had left London and, with their equally dedicated elders in Union Movement, had harvested another crop of converts in Southend.

When I showed Max and Alexander what I'd written they made it clear they would both like to leave the room to be sick.

There was another, more serious, side to both of them, however. 'The trouble is,' Max said one day in my room, 'Union Movement is made up of a bunch of clowns who aren't serious about achieving power. They just want to hang around pubs and talk about the old days and how good they were at beating up Jews. When I pointed out to you on the phone that there were five million teenagers in Britain, Trevor, I was talking about the vast potential political power of the young. Apart from their spending power, they could change the face of Britain if they were mobilised by some political force. But where's the appeal of Don Lucas, Derek Ashton with his pictures of Hitler, and all the others who are so out-of-touch and remote from what's going on in the coffee shops, pubs, restaurants and clubs?' He was polite enough not to include me. 'The Teddy Boys would be a better bet than the lot we've got. If he went political, Elvis Presley could be the next President of the United States. What Union Movement needs is people like Marty Wilde.' He asked me to put on the sensation of 1957, 'Jailhouse Rock' and performed a staggering imitation of Elvis. He told me that his father and mother adored the American singer. 'Dad's favourite is "I don't care if the sun don't shine".'

Dad? I wanted to interrupt and say, 'Do you mean The Leader?'

When I told him that the lower and upper sixths of Archbishop Tenison's had formed a skiffle group called The Harlequins, and that I had been asked to play in it because I had studied music and played the violin, Max's eyes opened wide. He said that he could organise a massive party at an empty flat he knew in Victoria. It was close to the station and 302. Could I pass the word around and persuade young people to come? There must be dozens of boys I knew at Tenison's and if each one of them knew five boys and five girls . . . It was before the days of pocket calculators but Max carried one around in his head.

Having a series of parties, he said, would be the right way to get in with lively, ordinary, normal young people, girls as well as boys, and attract them to the Movement by showing that we were like them and didn't go on about Hitler and Mussolini, Franco and British Fascism all the time.

Both Max and Alexander wanted to meet young Jews, and Alexander was delighted when I told him about my, now distant, friend, the half-Jewish Timothy who still lived at the end of Blandford Square.

I hardly ever saw Tim because of my own obsession with Union Movement, but had heard he was having difficulty keeping up socially with the other boys at Haberdashers Askes. He felt the pain of moving from one social class to another without sufficient money to soften the transition. When we were still close friends, he'd told me that he didn't like inviting boys from Haberdashers to his pokey top-floor flat. Other boys, he said, lived in vast houses near Hampstead Heath, St John's Wood, Golders Green or places like Richmond and Hampton Court.

I said to Max and Alexander that I'd invite Tim over to meet them. 'Have the boys gone?' asked my mother when she heard the door close. 'They're a credit to their father, Max and Ali. They seem to want to know everything about what it was like in the old days, and what Old Members think Mosley should be doing now. It's wonderful you've formed such a close friendship with The Leader's sons, Trevor.' She seemed totally unaware that there might be financial or class differences involved which would stop a real friendship developing.

I put my arms around her and gave her a hug and she clung to me and said, 'Don't let me down, Trevor. Don't let me down. Now that the rector has gone you're my only hope left, Trevor. My only hope left.'

I noticed as I held her that she had placed a framed picture of me speaking at Trafalgar Square next to the fencing picture of The Leader. I felt frightened.

A decision to change my ways and become a normal 1957 teenager led to my inclusion in The Harlequins as a regular guitarist. Practice sessions took place once a week at the home of a boy called Frost, who lived close to Dulwich. Having finished paying for my Johnnie Ray jacket, I opened an account with a music shop in Edgware Road and started paying every month for a steel-stringed 'Spanish' guitar.

Within a few weeks I had mastered the three main chords necessary for such songs as Lonnie Donnegan's 'Midnight Special', 'Rock Island Line', and others which included 'Ain't You Glad', 'Cumberland Gap' and 'It Takes a Worried Man To Sing a Worried Song'.

I was uncomfortable at the beginning because the boys in the group knew I had some connection with a strange political movement. But the boy on the washboard with his mum's thimbles on his fingers,

Fisher of 6A, broke the ice. When we reached a line which said:

> *I saw Peter, Paul and Moses*
> *Playing ring around the roses.*

He diplomatically and humorously sung instead:

> *I saw Peter, Paul and Mosley*
> *Playing ring around the rosary.*

And that was it. I was in and no one mentioned my Fascist connections. I think for the first time in my life I asked myself, Well, just what is Fascism, or Sir Oswald Mosley to these people who want to have a good time after school and homework; who just want to enjoy themselves with their guitars bought on hire purchase, their tea-chests and washboards, and pretty little, or not so little, pony-tailed girlfriends from South London who idolise them while they sing? After all, if Max and Alexander, The Leader's sons, said I was mad not to take advantage of London and have a good time while I was young . . .

I very much wanted a girlfriend to sing to. I would sing and stare at her and not care if she got pregnant.

Within three weeks, my prayed-for Madonna came onto the scene, a twenty-five-year-old girl from Dulwich called Sonia Marchand. She said she was half-Scottish and half-Italian. She had black hair down to her waist, heavily made-up dark brown eyes which anticipated the fashion revolution of the next decade, a figure like an hour-glass, and clothes like some avant-garde painter or novelist from Ernest Hemingway's Paris of the 1920s. She was on the point of divorce, having been married for less than two years. Her French accountant husband was planning to go to live in Canada where, after a suitable break, she might or might not join him.

Sonia Marchand had wandered into a café in Wardour Street where The Harlequins were auditioning for a one-night stand. Our temporary manager, lead singer and tea-chest player, Frostie, said we didn't want money, just as much coffee as we could swallow and a spaghetti at the end of the session. 'Not asking much, are you?' said the spiv who ran the shop. 'I'll give you a try but I'm telling you now if you make too much noise you're out on your ear and no arguing.' In the event we played there for a fortnight before being asked to depart by public request.

Sonia Marchand introduced herself and her wealthy-looking companion, who said he was a banker. After ten minutes she asked me for my telephone number and said she would ring me, which left the rest of the group a helpless heap of envy.

'You lucky bastard, Grundy,' said Micky Barrell, a schoolfriend who'd left Tenison's at fifteen to join the print. He wanted to be our business manager. 'That's about the best-looking bird I've ever seen in my life. What's she see in you, for Christ's sake.'

'Must be the eyes,' said Fisher. 'Look at his eyes. All sad and sincere. Can't be his guitar playing 'cos that's bloody awful.' And he sang:

> *We all realise*
> *That it must be his eyes*
> *'Cos his guitar playing's bloody awful.*

'About as good as your lyrics,' I said to Fisher, who threw one of his thimbles at me.

I was rapidly tiring of A level school work, mainly because I was useless at geography and found it almost impossible to tolerate the ravings of the senior history teacher, Birchenough, the man who caned people with DAs or Tony Curtis haircuts.

Birchenough seemed to have returned from the war a lonely, embittered man who likened anyone in history he did not like or understand to Adolf Hitler. Hence, Louis XIV had 'Hitlerite' tendencies and so did Gustavus Adolphus and Richelieu. Anyone who seemed to have made up their mind where they were going in life was a Nazi-type. The school was led and instructed by men who had undergone shattering experiences in the war, but under the regime of Dr Punch, himself a survivor of the First War as well as the Second, they were not allowed to talk about those experiences, or even say how they felt about the future. Only our English teacher, a solid, square, tough-looking man, called Farrell, spoke to us during lessons about what it had been like during the Second World War.

Farrell had been an officer with the Gurkhas in Burma. Towards the end of the war he'd been in France and had married a French woman. I asked him if it was true that the Germans in France had been as bad as they were portrayed.

'Much worse,' he said.

'But did you see atrocities or was that just propaganda?'

'You can have no idea how vile they were, Grundy, and yet I am told that you sympathise with the Hitler people. How can you, an intelligent boy, sympathise with such monsters? Who is getting at you? That's what I want to know. Who is getting at you? You must break away from them. You must. Otherwise, those Mosley people will destroy you. And after all the Germans did to the French, your hero Oswald Mosley has gone to live in France. They must be even more tolerant or stupid than I thought.'

I had respect for this man and didn't argue with him. I started to realise how widespread the knowledge was at Archbishop Tenison's that I was a Mosleyite.

I told Jeffrey Hamm what Farrell had said.

'The man is probably a Communist. A lot of well-meaning English liberals relate to France because of its so-called respect for intellectuals. But the tolerance is skin deep. Skin deep.'

He went upstairs and came down with a book which he said I must first read then review for *Union*. It was Sisley Huddleston's *France: The Tragic Years*. 'No relation to the ghastly Trevor Huddleston, thank the Lord,' Hamm said. He spoke to me as an equal, a fellow who had shared the platform with him at Trafalgar Square. 'Don't be taken in by Communist schoolteachers, Trevor, even though they are teaching sixth-form literature. I was a teacher once in Wales and the whole profession is riddled with fellow travellers. The Communists don't go for numbers, they don't try and get people into the Communist Party. They convert people and then tell them to keep away from the Party and work in the trade unions, the schools, the churches. Your Mr Farrell is probably one of those. Read this and you'll understand what happened in France. The French called back the old war hero Pétain to lead them and he knew that fighting Hitler was ridiculous, so he did what any decent patriot would have done, he reached a compromise with Hitler and an honourable settlement with the Germans.

'And when the rats came out of the sewers led by General de Gaulle – who is right now being acclaimed a hero because he is going to sell out France and give Algeria to the Reds – they put Pétain on trial, even though he was an old man in his eighties. Do you know that when France was liberated by the Allies and the likes of your Mr Farrell, more people were killed for supporting the Germans than were killed during the entire French Revolution?'

I was a little bitter that Mr Farrell had lied to me. Why hadn't he mentioned Pétain? Did only Mosley and his followers know anything at all about European history and what happened in the war? I made a note to ask Jeffrey Hamm if, had Hitler invaded England in 1940, The Leader would also have co-operated with the Germans? I wrote in an exercise book, 'Would OM have been like Pétain?' and circled it.

Before I left headquarters that afternoon, Jeffrey said to me, 'Oh, and by the way, Trevor, I think that music is a good thing and that it's right for you to mix with young people outside the Movement, but don't forget your first duty, will you? You have an example to set. I've been told that you've started to spend more time with a skiffle group in West End cafés than with your youth movement. And I had a look at your sales figures for last week . . . They're terrible.'

On the way home that night I bumped into Father Crisp, who was delivering his parish paper and circulating pamphlets advertising a meeting of the Campaign for Nuclear Disarmament at St Mark's the following week. My mother, Lovene and I had stopped attending church and there had been no mention of my becoming a vicar for several months.

'You should be doing this, Trevor Grundy, and not wasting any more time with that horrible man Oswald Mosley,' Father Crisp said to me. 'You'll fail your A levels, not get into a college and what then? What then?' In a singsong voice, as he walked away and towards another letter box, he said, 'You can't be a Christian and a Fascist at the same time,' and then a little louder. 'Do you hear me, Trevor Grundy? You can't be a Christian and a Fascist at the same time.'

In my room I sat by the open window and stared outside at the wall which seemed to be moving closer and closer towards me. I opened *Northanger Abbey*, which was an A level set book. The following day I had to read the preface to the class. One of the boys had underlined a sentence in red ink. It read, 'When Jane was sixteen she grew her hair and longed for balls.' Was I laughing or crying when I closed the book and rolled onto my narrow bed to stare up at the ceiling? 'What am I going to do with the rest of my life? I am no longer certain about anything, not even Mosley.'

My mother opened the door. 'Come and have a cup of tea if you're not doing your homework.' And then, 'Some lass called Sonia Something rang up and said would you ring her. Said it was something to do with a charity concert in Dulwich.' She closed the door and then opened it again. 'You're going to get yourself into a real mess,' she said. 'Oh, and a friend of Freddie Shepherd's rang and said the Sunday meeting has been cancelled. And Les Smith's mother telephoned. Someone has hit him and he's gone to Paddington Hospital.'

I went to Les's house and his mother opened the door. She was Irish and quite a heavy woman. I saw the face of one of Les's pretty, dark-haired, ivory-skinned sisters peering at me from behind a door. With eye contact, she disappeared.

Mrs Smith let me have it: 'You're a bad young man and you're a terrible influence on Leslie. He's been in trouble before and you knew that and now look what's happened.' I thought she was going to hit me. 'You've introduced him to a collection of hooligans in Islington and he's been trying to get his own sisters to join your God-forsaken Union Movement, or whatever it's called. That Mosley man is evil

136

and I'm saying to you, Trevor Grundy, you should stop this nonsense and leave Leslie and the rest of my family alone. Do you hear me? Alone! You're still at school and you should be studying, not standing shouting on street corners about things you know nothing about. Do you hear me? Know nothing about!'

I asked if I could see Les.

'You can but for the last time in this house. The last time. Do you hear me? The very last time!'

Les was in bed and I could hardly see his eyes. They were in the back of his head and terribly bruised.

'What the hell happened to you?' I asked. 'Who did this to you? Who did it? Was it the Communists? Have you been up to Islington? Does Freddie know?'

Les said nothing. His mouth was swollen, which made his lips seem enormous. He was crying. After a long silence, he said, 'It wasn't the Communists.'

I got closer to him because I found it hard to hear what he was saying.

'It wasn't them, it was our lot, Fred's mates,' and he named names which meant nothing to me.

'Do you want me to tell Jeffrey Hamm? I'll go down now to 302 and tell him. He'll do something. I tell you, Les. Jeffrey Hamm will do something!'

'Don't tell the bloody police and don't tell Jeffrey Hamm or anyone else in this bloody Movement. And you! You can sod off! You're a bloody little Mummy's boy and you don't know anything about anything, and you don't know what this bloody Movement is about and who runs it and what's going on. They're a bunch of bloody queers from top to bottom. Look at me! Look at me! I've had it, I'm finished. Leave me alone! I don't want to see you or anyone else in this bloody lunatic Movement ever again!' He sat up. 'Do you hear me, I say!' Then, in a long-hidden, thick Southern Irish accent, 'Do you hear me is all I've got left to say to you, Trevor-bloody-goody-two-shoes-bloody-Grundy.'

When I left, Mrs Smith slammed the door. I turned to take a last look at the boarding house and saw a sister peering at me until she closed the curtain.

Later I spoke to Fred's sidekick, a tall, seedy, greasy, dirty, dangerous man in his late twenties or early thirties, called Greg.

'Don't talk to me about what happened to that little sod Les Smith. He's been taking Freddie for a ride long enough. He was supposed to meet us at the pub and was late. I came back to the office to see what we'd taken selling our stuff in the market and what did I see? Who did I see, rather? Les Smith helping himself to the money in Freddie's bleedin' desk, didn't I? With my own eyes! So some of us decided to take the law into our own hands and we gave Mister Leslie bleedin' Smith what he's been asking for, for a long time, ever since I can remember. And I suggest you keep your bleedin' big nose out of things and go and say your prayers in church and hope it doesn't happen to you. We've had enough of you poncy little shits running around on the platform with everyone at 302 saying, "Why can't you do more for the Movement like Trevor Grundy and Les Smith?" '

I could hear anger and violence bubbling in his voice.

'Freddie said to me only last night, "Greg," he said, "those kids are burning themselves out and when they've gone we'll still be here, won't we? We'll always be with the Old Man, even though those kids won't." '

'Les is in a terrible state,' I said. 'Can I speak to Fred? I need to tell him just how bad. I mean, Fred can't just say he's not responsible.'

'Sod off,' said Greg. 'Freddie doesn't know and if there's anyone going to tell him, well, I wouldn't like to be in his shoes, would you?'

The phone went dead and for a few minutes so did I.

Sonia telephoned several times before I found the courage to walk down to Marylebone Station to ring the number she had given me. A voice said, 'Mrs Marchand.'

'This is Trevor, Trevor Grundy. We met at the café with the skiffle group and you telephoned me and . . .'

'Do you want to speak to Sonia?' came the smiling voice. 'This is her mother-in-law, Eileen Marchand.'

Sonia laughed. 'It took you long enough to pick up the phone, didn't it? Scared?'

'No, not at all but I've been tied up for the last couple of days and . . .'

'There's no need to be scared,' said Sonia. 'I just want to see you, to talk to you. Ronnie Fisher, your sweet washboard player with all the thimbles, lives in the same block of flats as we do . . . as I do . . . and he told me that at last you've come out of your cocoon and have started to do the normal sort of things people do at your age. He told me that you're a supporter of Oswald Mosley. I've read quite a lot about him. I'd love to talk to you. I'd like to get to know you. Interested?'

I only had ninepence. It would be embarrassing if I couldn't put more money in the box, so I had to hurry.

'Yes, well, I mean, why not? Yes. I mean, I don't know much about Mosley, or anything really but . . .'

It kept going through my head, you're not yet eighteen and she told Fisher she was twenty-five, but that could mean older. God, say she was twenty-six? And she's married. The only girl I'd ever been near in my life was Angela Watson, the auburn-haired fifteen-year-old daughter of Jimmy Watson, branch leader of Woolwich. I'd danced with her at a Movement dinner eighteen months before. 'No, I'd like to, but you'll have to say where because it would be a bit difficult round here because . . .'

'Stop being so evasive and non-committal,' she said. 'I'm not going to eat you. My husband, Yvan, is here if that makes you feel any better. Would you like to speak to him?'

'No,' I said, 'I'm not at all scared and I don't want to speak . . .'

'Hello Trevor,' came the voice. 'Sonia says you're a fascinating young man and that you'll come and have supper with us here one evening next week, so please make arrangements. I hope to see something of you before I go to Canada for our trial separation.' He laughed.

'There,' said Sonia, 'you're invited.' She told me how to get to her flat. 'But you know where. Where Ronnie Fisher lives. They're on the second floor and we're on the third. There are buses back to the Oval every twenty minutes after ten o'clock and you can come after school.'

Fisher told me that Sonia's husband had left for Canada the day of the call. And what sort of man was it who'd tell a complete stranger that he was having a trial separation from his wife? And the mother lived there as well. I wasn't scared. I was terrified.

That night I told Alexander Mosley what had happened. He was now a regular visitor to the house, pampered always by my mother, who remarked on his stunning resemblance to The Leader. I saw how much that annoyed him, but he said nothing to her.

He told me in my room, where the large portrait of his father looked down on him, 'I didn't know what to make of your family. But I can see that your mother is very sincere about Dad. It's sad, tragic even.'

'Sad? Tragic? We're lucky to know him and support him,' I said. 'Think of supporting Harold Macmillan or that bloke who runs the Labour Party.'

Alexander changed the subject and was delighted to hear about Sonia Marchand.

'In France, young men of a certain class and age are taken by their fathers to a brothel and left there for the afternoon. Not left in the care, as it were, of some insensitive tart, but perhaps one of their father's old regulars. It happens, you know. They're very gentle, very understanding and afterwards you're regarded as a man. It makes it all so much easier than the way other sections of society deal with sex, all the dishonesty, all those lies, the awful fumbling.

'Certain African tribes use the equivalent of the French system. In fact, the Masai put their teenagers in the care of aunts and uncles and they see to all the sex bit. Perhaps I should tell Jeffrey Hamm about it and he could write an article for the *European* for my mother: "Puberty, the English working-class sexual revolution, Mosley and the Masai." Can't you see it?' He roared with laughter, rolled his eyes and pretended to write an article. He mimed an African elder and a virgin going to a brothel. I thought he was possibly a little mad, but

140

quite the most fascinating person I had ever met.

'You must go and see your Sonia Marchand and let it happen if it's going to happen. How old are you, seventeen and three-quarters? I'd say about time. Way beyond about time in my opinion.'

I wished Alexander would come with me for supper in Dulwich and organise it so it would be painless. Or, better still, that I could be enrolled in some African society and sealed away in a hut until I was twenty and not have to speak at street corners any more or sell *Union* or worry about Les Smith, who hadn't phoned or contacted me since the night of the beating-up, or worry about sex and being a virgin, which seemed to be a terrible disease. In a sealed hut I wouldn't have to worry any more about geography, Father Crisp, what I was going to do after school if I failed my A levels or whether I was still destined to become the Mosley of the Anglican Church or just an ordinary schoolteacher.

But the conversation with Alexander had cleared my head and put lead into a nervous pencil. Instead of going to have supper with Sonia and her husband, I would daringly ask her to come with me to the party that Max was throwing in Victoria the following week. Max had predicted, in his impeccable cockney, the accent nearly all the sixth-formers at Archbishop Tenison's were trying to lose, that it would be the biggest rock and roll gathering ever seen in London and would probably go on all night.

Sweet lord, wouldn't they be impressed when I turned up with twenty-five- or twenty-six-year-old, long-haired, dark-eyed, soft-lipped Sonia from Dulwich? That would stop Max treating me like a retarded curate.

On the advice of Jeffrey Hamm, I took Derek to a Paddington café and asked him to stop telling people that the real leader of Union Movement was Adolf Hitler's ghost. Derek had become a deeply disturbed young man. I had now asked him to stop saying that, not once but four times, and so I finally told him that he should go to 302 to have a chat with Jeffrey Hamm. Jeffrey expelled him from the Movement.

He said that it had hurt him because Derek was very sincere about his beliefs and would probably drift towards one of the 'fringe' organisations which were starting to build up in memory of William Joyce, who'd broadcast to Britain from Germany during the war as Lord Haw-Haw.

Without my old faithfuls like Les and Derek standing around me I felt strangely alone at the Praed Street meetings. Since Alexander and Max had so suddenly and unsettlingly entered my narrow world, I felt decidedly awkward standing on a platform on a Saturday afternoon, when there were so many good-looking girls walking past, totally ignoring me and what I had to say.

For my contemporaries, Saturday afternoons were for shopping and putting on headsets in Church Street market to hear the latest records from America and from the growing stable of musical talent in Britain. Oswald Mosley? Hardly any member of my age group had heard of him, and what they had heard, at a time when the popular press was telling the heroic story of Anne Frank for the first time, disgusted them.

At the end of my 138th meeting Don Lucas said to me, 'You've lost interest, haven't you, Trev? So many people said it would happen but I didn't want to believe it. Not you.'

His mouth was slightly open and, with his white shirt, black tie, and his flash-and-circle belt buckle, he looked like a washing-powder salesman on television. Perhaps he would fly away with a packet of soapflakes in his hand towards the dirtier parts of Britain, so he could make them sparklingly, dazzlingly, shiningly Mosley clean.

'Of course I haven't lost interest, Don,' I lied. 'How could I? Mosley and the Movement mean everything to me. It's just, well, we can't carry on with the Dereks of this world, can we? I mean, there's a new age now. Young people don't want to spend hours talking about Hitler and Rudolf Hess. Those days have gone. We've got to have a new recruiting system.'

I must have looked at my watch because Don went to the pub. I folded up the black platform with 'Mosley Youth' painted in red letters on it and walked back to Blandford Square to get ready for the rock and roll party of the year. The only question I had on my brain was, will Sonia turn up?

Disappointment registered all over Max's face. By eleven fifteen there were ten people in a very large, unfurnished but potentially luxurious flat, which was little more than a stone's throw from the walls of Buckingham Palace. The ten included six half-baked musicians who made up The Harlequins.

To my surprise, at eleven thirty Alexander Mosley walked in with Timothy Adams, who was about the same height and build as The Leader's son. Max and Alex had met Tim during a skiffle practice session at my house. If The Leader's sons liked skiffle, then the front room was available to The Harlequins, said my mother. Alex and Tim spent a long time sitting in a corner, talking earnestly to one another. Occasionally, Max would join in the conversation and the three would laugh loudly.

I had brought along a half-bottle of Scotch in my guitar case. We sang songs, the usual skiffle repertoire, and when we had a break for drinks I opened my expensive bottle with pride. I swallowed the equivalent of two doubles in one go, controlled an almost immediate desire to be sick and looked at my audience with a nonchalant 'Oh, I do that every half hour' look on my face.

I had only been drunk once before. After a successful speech in Praed Street, I'd gone to a pub in Dorset Square with Les Smith and Derek Ashton. I consumed six pints of bitter, tripped over the kerb and fell flat on my face. Derek helped me up and his face registered disgust. He was a teetotaller and vegetarian. He looked at me and said with Welsh music in his voice, 'Trevor, you're drunk. What would the Führer say? What *would* the Führer say?'

The London jazz clubs shut down around midnight, so by one o'clock in the morning Max Mosley's prediction that this would be the rock and roll party of the year wasn't far off. By two o'clock, I think there must have been close on a couple of hundred youths scattered throughout the flat, many a bit intoxicated, some hopelessly drunk. There was, in that flat, the largest gathering of girls I'd ever been in the presence of in my life. Until then, the only time I'd seen a large group of females had been at a fifth-form dance to which girls from two south London grammar schools had been invited. They'd worn dresses, flat shoes and ponytails. We'd hardly touched as we'd danced and had been under the ever-watchful eyes of schoolmasters and mistresses. The girls at this party were different, alien visitors from outside my planetary system. Some were sixth-formers but most were secretaries, or students from Central St Martin's School of Art, the Royal Academy of Dramatic Art or the Swiss Cottage Central School of Speech and Drama. Most had come with their boyfriends, or boys who had picked them up that night, and were wearing skin-tight jeans and T-shirts with the CND symbol. When they danced, they jived or skipped around the room and when there were slow numbers they pushed their bodies hard up against their boyfriend's. This was no fifth-form treat. I felt utterly out of place as Max took to the floor with an attractive, but rather hard-faced girl who looked as if she was going to make love to him standing up. And they had known one another only for a few minutes.

I watched him talk and whisper and had the distinct impression he wasn't telling her about his relationship to Sir Oswald or trying to explain why young people should join the Youth League and help to sell *Union* papers at Earl's Court Underground Station on a Saturday night.

By three o'clock, the noise was almost unbearable and I was called by one of the skiffle group to the front door. Three policemen were standing there.

'Who's in charge here?' asked a constable.

'I am,' said Max.

'Well, you're making an awful lot of noise. You'll turn down that music. We've had complaints. Lots of complaints.'

Max replied that the music was not loud and that young people had every right to have a party on a Saturday night and make a noise. That earned him a loud cheer from those leaning out of the windows to see what was going on. 'That's right, Max! You tell 'em, mate! It's only the bleedin' law, that's what it is.'

The policemen appeared to be a little intimidated but Max did agree to see that the record player was turned down. As soon as he saw the policemen cycle away, he turned it up again and told everyone to make as much noise as they wanted. That earned another cheer and I heard someone say, 'Good bloke, Max. Who is he?'

By four o'clock the police had returned and about twenty-five people crowded around the front door to see what would happen. It was the same conversation. Max promised to end the party at six o'clock. The police left.

One of the Harlequins took me to one side. 'There's some poor old sod who lives upstairs with his wife,' he said. 'He's just told me that the owners of the place are trying to get him and his old lady out, but they've been paying next to nothing in rent and don't want to leave. Strikes me this bloody noise will drive them out. Is that why we're here, Trev?'

How could I tell him that the real reason, as I understood it, was to recruit young people into Union Movement?

At six o'clock, as promised, we started to drift off home. I was very drunk, very tired and I felt at least another three spots coming up around the back of my neck. It was only as I crossed the cobbled area between the flat and the main road that I realised Sonia hadn't turned up.

Max organised another party at the flat for the following week. Even more artists, musicians, students and secretaries, with and without boyfriends showed up. The Harlequins were given the slow handclap and asked not to play. More skilled fingers, better voices, coming from faces which looked much more like James Dean's, had taken over. Some of the new groups had played at the Two Is, some at Cy Laurie's. St Mark's Church Hall no longer counted.

Again the police appeared but went away after being told that the flat was not empty but was lived in by a group of musicians and that the law about holding a party was on our side.

Around six o'clock on the morning of the last party, as we prepared to go home, Timothy Adams, now a constant companion of

145

Alexander and Max, told me that he had been asked not only to join the Movement but to lead its youth wing. Would I stay in a branch led by him? He told me that no one supported me and that I had only ever attracted a dozen or so social misfits.

Timothy Adams, half-Jewish Little John to my Robin Hood, dared to talk to me like this. Where were my arrows?

'I'm a firm believer in what Mosley says about European union,' Timothy asserted. 'My parents are wrong to say Mosley's anti-Jewish. It might even be announced in *Union* that the new youth leader of Union Movement is Jewish . . .' He went off with Alexander and a starlet-looking girl.

Bewildered and lonely, I took my guitar, as I had once taken my violin, and walked from the now silent flat towards the bus which would take me back to my safe world at 40 Blandford Square.

As I approached the bus stop, with tears starting to well up in my eyes, I heard the hoot of a car and turned to see who was trying to run me down in the early morning rain.

'Don't look so tragic,' said Sonia Marchand. 'You can't have played that badly.'

She opened the door and I sat beside her admiring her olive skin, black eyebrows and well-shaped nose, mouth and jawline. Her curtain of black hair fell way beyond her shoulders and looked lovely against a sky-blue sweater. She was wearing blue shorts, a white cotton shirt and, apart from the blue sweater around her shoulders, nothing else, not even shoes or sandals.

'Coffee at my flat and some breakfast and I should imagine by the smell and look of you, a bath and a sleep.'

As we turned right into Buckingham Palace Road I saw five figures walking arm-in-arm down the road, Max, Alexander, two gorgeous girls and Timothy Adams. We stopped at the lights and we looked at each other but no one waved.

I left Sonia's flat at eight fifteen on Monday morning and closed the door softly. As I was tiptoeing down the flight of stairs I bumped into Fisher who was on his way to school. I was impressed by his smartness, his well-brushed black blazer, sixth-form tie and totally stunned face, which was already showing signs of belonging to a well-mannered, well-ordered, greasy-pole climber. Fisher was determined to become a cartographer when he left Tenison's in June 1958 after, probably, doing brilliantly in his two A levels, geography and art.

'What on earth are you doing here?' As he had caught me coming down the stairs from Sonia's top-floor flat, he didn't really need to ask.

I asked him in a man-to-man voice to be a mate and not tell anybody at school. 'I'll get my mother to ring up and say I've gone down with a bilious attack but, please, don't say anything to anyone.'

I noticed his pace increase as he approached the bus stop, where he turned round and said, 'Lucky bastard. Jeez, Grundy, it's time I got going.'

I had a feeling that Fisher was not to be trusted and that by the ten o'clock milk and bun break exaggerated stories about Grundy's sensational seduction of Dulwich's most eligible nymphomaniac would be all round the sixth form, seeping through to Dr Punch's MI5-like headquarters by lunchtime.

When I got back home, I found I had forgotten my key. My mother opened the door with a semi-tragic look on her face. She was fifty years of age. Wearing the headscarf she wore to do the housework, she looked like the woman at the well who had a long conversation with Jesus. I thought, Sonia will look like you when she's older.

'Where'veyoubeen?' She said it as one word.

'Look, Mum, it's too complicated to explain and I want to have a bath and sleep because I'm not feeling well.'

She closed the door. I knew she was delighted that I was home. An hour later she brought me in a cup of tea and said that the phone hadn't stopped ringing all Sunday afternoon and evening.

'Alexander Mosley and some giggling lasses. One of them asked to speak to Anthony Perkins. Was that supposed to be you?'

Alexander came round that evening and lolled back in the chair with a highly amused and approving look on his face. He looked like a young version of his father, whose portrait in black fencing jacket

147

looked down on both of us from the mantelpiece, over my book collection, which included Hitler's *Mein Kampf*, Mussolini's *My Life*, Alexander Raven's *Civilisation as Divine Superman* and two huge tomes entitled *Horrors from the Spanish Civil War* which acted as bookends.

'Well,' he said, like the imagined upper-class French father. 'What happened?'

In those days, I believed that when you asked a friend not to repeat a confidence, the secret would be as safe as money in a Post Office account.

'Of course, I won't tell anyone. Who's there to tell? But what happened? Suddenly she appeared, you were in her car looking damned smirky, I must say, and you didn't even stop to say hello. You were gone.'

'It was a nightmare,' I said. 'A nightmare.'

Alexander sat up. 'A nightmare? What on earth do you mean, a nightmare? How could it have been a nightmare? One of the most sensational girls in London picks you up in a car at six o'clock on an abysmal Sunday morning in London and you describe it as a nightmare?'

Sonia had taken me back to her flat and explained that she had not wanted to go to any of the parties because she'd felt she had nothing in common with anyone there, apart from me. But then she hardly knew me. And she had telephoned, but every time the phone had been answered by a gruff, aggressive, male voice which said, 'Who's that?' and then put the phone down. Fisher had told her what time we all went home from the parties so she had known where and when to pick me up that morning.

When we got back to her flat, she told me that her husband had left for Canada and that the trial separation had begun. As far as she was concerned, it would be for good. She'd left school at seventeen to live with Yvan, she said, but life had become flat and boring. Recently, she'd met a crowd of young graduates from London University, including an aspiring playwright who wanted to write a BBC drama on alienation. Sonia had told him about her brief meeting with The

148

Harlequins and how a Mosley-supporter was playing the guitar in the group and was still at school, a Church of England grammar school and he'd asked if she could arrange a meeting. Partly, that's why she had forced herself on me but, she added, only partly.

Alexander returned to his lolling position but now with a concerned expression on his good-looking face.

'And?'

'I went to sleep and the next thing I knew it was seven o'clock on Sunday evening. She told me to put on one of her husband's shirts, some socks and underpants, because we were going out for a meal. The playwright had fallen off his motorbike and couldn't come with us but would see us later that week.'

'There's no playwright,' said Alexander.

'No,' I said. 'I distinctly remember her saying that there was a playwright.'

After the meal and a bottle of wine, which she paid for, at a French restaurant in Dulwich Village, we returned to Sonia's flat. I was still quite drunk from the party and trying to cope with the fresh intake of alcohol. She poured me what I thought to be a giant-sized cognac and had one herself.

She put on some Italian music, took hold of my hand and asked me to dance with her. She danced in the silent but aggressive way I had seen others dance. When the record ended, she led me into her bedroom and we lay next to one another. Both of us were smoking cigarettes. Then she stood up, left the room and came back in the shorts and shirt she had picked me up in that morning. She looked at me for a long time and then slowly took her shirt off.

'That's when it happened, Alexander, that's when it happened. It was absolutely awful but I think, thank God, you'll understand.'

Alexander shot up again. 'What was awful? What was absolutely awful? How on earth can any of this be absolutely awful? Are you insane?'

'Around her neck,' I said. 'Around her neck she was wearing a gold chain, and hanging from it, you're not going to believe this, a Star of David. Can you imagine? She's Jewish. I was in bed with a married

Jewish woman who had around her neck a Star of David. I pushed her away from me and went back to the room where I'd been sleeping, locked the door and the next thing I knew it was six o'clock in the morning, Monday morning, this morning.

'I had a horrendous headache because of the party and then the bottle of wine, and I wanted to talk to her but there was no reply when I knocked on her bedroom door, so I waited until eight fifteen and that's when I left.'

Alexander stared in blank disbelief. 'You mean to say you pushed aside a semi-naked Sonia Marchand, one of the most beautiful girls I have seen in London, because she had a Star of David around her neck. Oh God,' he said, 'Oh God. I am in pain, deep, deep pain.'

I watched him roll around in the chair. He started to speak in Spanish, or Italian, I couldn't tell. It sounded like a prayer.

My mother opened the door. 'Would you boys like a cup of tea?'

After a long and now, on my part, embarrassed silence, tea came. I said to Alexander, 'I couldn't have. I mean it would have been letting down The Leader, I mean letting your father down. And can you imagine the repercussions if she had got herself pregnant?'

He stared at me with a look of bemused contempt. 'My father would have ravished her. I would have ravished her. Everyone in the whole world would have ravished her, apart from you. You're insane. Hopelessly and utterly insane.'

8

Sid Proud's telephone call to my mother, on my eighteenth birthday, changed my life.

'Mrs Grundy,' he said – and the fact that he spoke to my mother showed me clearly for the first time that in the eyes of most people I hardly existed. At best I was a pawn on a chessboard controlled by my mother – 'Mrs Grundy, an amazing job opportunity has come up at Spanish Travel. I need a courier to travel from London to Port Bou, near Barcelona.

'I need a young, serious-minded, intelligent boy, and Alexander Mosley said to me that Trevor needs a long break out of England, and what with Trevor's excellent Movement background . . . It's such an opportunity for Trevor, Mrs Grundy.

'It's ten pounds a week, all expenses paid, but there'll be plenty of tips at the end of holidays, provided the punters like what he does for them.

'He can take all his books down to Spain with him and study for his A levels in his free time. What's more, he'll probably return at the end of the season, that's mid-October, Mrs Grundy, fluent in Spanish and French. It's a great opportunity.'

My mother brought the news to me as I lay in bed. My first thoughts were, How can I survive away from her, away from the Movement, so far from Blandford Square?

'But school? What about school?' I protested weakly. 'I mean, I'm

151

supposed to take my exams in June and it's mid-March now.'

My mother looked up at Mosley with her 'give-me-strength' look. I thought she might cross herself. She handed me a birthday card from her and my father, whom I rarely saw these days, as he was always out in his cab. 'You can take them at Christmas. What's a few months if you can learn Spanish and French?' She took my hand and held it quite tightly. 'I've only ever wanted to go to two places in my life, Spain and Egypt. I feel as if I'm really from one of those two places and not from England at all, especially not from Seaton Sluice or Whitley Bay. I feel this isn't really where I should be living and that – it's hard to say – in my soul I should be a gypsy with Spaniards around me, or in a bazaar bargaining or listening to wise men talking about Jesus and God, not this,' she said. 'Not this.'

She stood up, still a striking figure in her working scarf and pinafore. She saluted Mosley's picture and it reminded me of the days when she used to salute me, an eleven-year-old Tenisonian marching off to Marylebone Underground Station at eight o'clock every morning, satchel bumping up and down.

'You can pay for me to come to Spain with you and that will make up for everything,' she said.

That was it, I thought. Get dressed, go to school and tell Birchenough and Dr Punch that I won't be taking my exams in June.

At school, having bidden an emotional goodbye to the masters, I waited downstairs to say goodbye to The Harlequins, but only Fisher appeared. He opened his black briefcase and gave me a brown envelope, which I could feel contained a book.

'I'm sorry you're leaving,' he said. 'Came as a bit of a surprise. Now we've got to get another guitarist. Shouldn't be hard to find someone as good as you.' He was smiling. 'This is from Mrs Marchand. Happy Birthday to you.'

On the Underground to Marylebone I opened the envelope and found a copy of J.D. Salinger's *The Catcher in the Rye*. I spotted the word *phoney* six times between the Oval and Waterloo, where I changed onto the Bakerloo line.

Inside the book was a letter from Sonia. 'The hero is a bit like you,' she wrote, 'always on the lookout for phoneys. Trevor, dearest Trevor, be careful you don't become one yourself.

'When you read this, I will be a long time gone, so don't get all phoney and say you're sad. Your mother won't be sad. If you had started to love me, your life would have changed, wouldn't it, and I don't think you would have had any time to sell your newspapers. Silly boy.

'You will be one of those young men in books who believe in things up to about the age of twenty-five or at the latest thirty. And then you will never believe in anything again.' She added a final 'never' and signed it just 'Sonia'.

She had not bothered to sign the book and I lost it a couple of weeks later.

When I asked Jeffrey Hamm about J.D. Salinger, he told me that *The Catcher in the Rye* was designed to muddle the minds of young people and that it was part of a 'let's confuse the youth' culture which was growing up around people like John Osborne and a few others who were branded 'angry young men' by the Jewish-controlled press.

'Keep your anger dry for when it's really needed,' Jeffrey told me. 'Don't be taken in by Jewish propaganda.'

Union Movement's dry anger was ignited a few weeks later, in April 1958, when the Campaign for Nuclear Disarmament held a large rally in Trafalgar Square. The rally was followed by a march from London to the Weapons Research Establishment, where about 12,000 demonstrators surrounded the complex at Aldermaston. One of the CND marchers was Nicholas Mosley and one of Union Movement's leading protesters was the well-known author's half-brother, Alexander.

Before we left 40 Blandford Square, *de facto* headquarters of Union Movement's youth brigade, we packed several cardboard cartons full of week-old eggs, rich and bad enough to throw at the Marxists and fellow travellers who would be trying to weaken Britain's defence system.

Alexander was passionate about the march and said we should hurl as much abuse and as many eggs as possible against the demonstrators. We planned to ambush them at Hammersmith Bridge.

I had returned as unofficial youth leader because Timothy had quarrelled with Max and Alexander about tactics. Timothy had fallen under the influence of a small group of people who hung around Sid Proud. They were what Union Movement members called 'the fringe', neo-Nazis officially scorned by Mosley, who described them as clowns and dwarfs, posing in the jackboots of dead giants. The neo-Nazis, in return, said that Mosley was a sell-out. Some even repeated claims made against him when he founded the British Fascists in 1932: that he was of Jewish origin, that his first wife, Cynthia Curzon, was Jewish and that Mosley was a 'kosher' Fascist, whose task was to attract all the extreme elements of the right-wing in Britain, march them to the nearest cliff and wave them goodbye.

In my room, before we left for Hammersmith, Alexander addressed a group of us, including my brother-in-law John and several of his Union Movement contemporaries. He urged us to adopt the Spanish Civil War slogan, 'They shall not pass', against the left-wing marchers.

They did pass, and in mighty numbers, but not before a few were splattered with rotten eggs and tomatoes. At one point, much to my amazement, I saw Alexander leave the Union Movement group and wave at one of the marchers. Was he going to attack the man? Instead, he joined in the walk to Aldermaston.

'Has Alexander gone insane?' asked one of the members.

'God knows,' I snapped. I felt confused and betrayed by Alexander's behaviour, and at the same time rather worried about him. I threw the rest of the eggs with even greater force.

Once the eggs were gone, we picked fights with members of the Hammersmith Communist Party and stole most of their rather expensive, well-made banners, which we bore triumphantly back to Blandford Square. In the basement, we took photographs of ourselves posing next to the woven slogans, which read, 'Workers of the world unite – you have nothing to lose but your chains.'

About a week later, Alexander rang the bell and came and sat miserably in my room. He explained that the man he'd waved to at the march was his brother, Nicholas. 'Nicholas is helping me see the world differently, Trevor. And he's helping with Dad. Dad wants me to be a chartered accountant but I want to go to university or to South America, I don't know.' The Leader was also putting pressure on Alexander over his relationship with Sid Proud's daughter, whom he obviously did not consider a suitable match. 'Maybe God does exist, after all, Trevor. You know, I've met some amazingly intelligent men who are senior members of the Anglican Church.'

But finding God didn't seem to make him in the slightest bit happier and he looked even more miserable when I told him, brightly, like some convert to the Billy Graham campaign then touring Britain, that I was really pleased because I had found God years ago at Christ Church.

'God will change your life, Al,' I told him.

He gave me one of his 'I'm about to be sick' looks and said he had to go and have supper with his mother and father at Cheyne Walk.

'Has Alexander gone?' my mother asked. 'He looks more and more like The Leader. Perhaps he'll be the next Leader when OM dies.'

I had never heard my mother acknowledge that one day Oswald Mosley would cease to walk the earth.

The following week we heard that the Communists and left-wing Labourites who were in control of King's Cross and St Pancras Council planned to fly the red flag over the Town Hall. I received a telephone call from headquarters asking me to turn up with a group of Union Movement members and speak against the Communists at the flag-raising ceremony. It was the weekend before my first trip to Spain.

I turned up opposite St Pancras Town Hall wearing the uniform white shirt, black tie and sixth-form blazer, minus the school badge, and mounted a wooden platform. A picture was published in *The Times* showing me ranting, raving and pointing my hand at a Communist speaker who, in turn, was ranting, raving and pointing at me.

It was the last time I ever spoke for Union Movement.

A copy of the picture was ordered from *The Times* by boys in Tenison's sixth-form, who stuck it up in their small common room next to the ground-floor lavatories.

One of the boys announced the formation of a new political party in memory of Hereward the Wake and named me as founder member. Letters were written by pupils of Tenison's to newspapers throughout south London advocating the repatriation of West Indians, Jews, the Irish and the Welsh, left-handed alcoholics and anyone who might offend conservative England.

I cycled over to the home of the boy I knew was responsible and wrote to one of the newspapers saying that I, Trevor Grundy, had never written letters or formed a movement in memory of Hereward the Wake.

A week later, the *Sunday Pictorial* carried a front page story on the sixth formers at Archbishop Tenison's who had caused so much confusion in the London press by claiming that a new ultra-right-wing party had been founded which wanted to send all West Indians home immediately.

I phoned Fisher about all this and he told me he never wanted to see me again. He said that Dr Robinson had suffered a mild heart attack but nobody knew whether it was connected with the *Sunday Pictorial* story which had brought disgrace to the school.

'A prefect's been ordered to remove a picture with you in it from a noticeboard,' Fisher said. 'And the junior boys have been told that you were expelled for unbecoming conduct.' It was a sadly fitting end to my inglorious career at Archbishop Tenison's.

I left England with a suitcase crammed full of A level text books so that I could study English literature, history and geography in Spain. I also had a Teach Yourself Spanish book from Foyles, a dictionary and a steel-stringed guitar.

At Victoria Station I waited for about thirty tourists, most of them elderly, but one of them a bright, fresh-faced schoolgirl aged sixteen, called Avril Hardy. She was travelling with her stern-faced father, Captain Hardy, who was the harbour-master at Ramsgate, her mother and her brother, a quiet, bespectacled, studious-looking boy of fourteen.

Travelling to Spain with us was Vivienne, a highly experienced courier who spoke several languages. Vivienne knew the ropes and wasn't going to tell me much, certainly nothing that would take francs and pesetas out of her pocket and put them into mine. My disadvantages were obvious and included an inability to speak either French or Spanish. 'Speak as much pidgin English as possible,' advised Vivienne, 'and most English people will think you're a linguist.'

I adjusted my Spanish Travel armband, picked up my suitcase and guitar and spent the next twenty-four hours getting myself to the tiny fishing harbour of Port Bou, first stop in Spain after the Pyrenees.

Apart from my suitcase, I carried a Gladstone bag packed full of pesetas bought by Spanish Travel at very favourable London prices. I didn't know it at the time, but I illegally shifted thousands of pounds' worth of pesetas into Spain during 1958 in order to pay Mr Proud's hotel and coach bills. Had I been caught, I suppose I would have been imprisoned, but it never happened mainly because, although Sid Proud hated Franco and Spanish Catholic Fascism – 'Pope's narks, the lot of them' – his business partners had good contacts in Barcelona and Madrid. These contacts received gifts from the London-based company which kept them sweet towards a little-known Irishman, who was doing the pioneering work of encouraging British holiday-makers to spend time and money in Franco's pariah state.

In Paris I was introduced to Spanish Travel's representative, André Négar. He was about forty-five and had fought with the Free French against the Germans during the Second World War. He told me that if he learnt to like me he would persuade Mr Proud to let me travel to Paris on business. I told him that my first love was history and that I had read a wonderful book by Sisley Huddleston about Marshal Pétain, which had told me all about the old man's amazing courage during the occupation.

'You're an ignorant but likeable idiot,' was his response.

Avril Hardy was no Sonia Marchand, but with her blue and white dress, her youthful, even boyish, haircut, fresh, smooth skin and large brown eyes, she looked a lot more manageable.

On the second night of her ten-day holiday in Port Bou, with its overcrowded and rather run-down Miramar Hotel, its U-shaped beach and restaurants which made me think I was walking into one of Vincent Van Gogh's night-time café pictures, I took Avril to the hills behind the coast. I kissed her and told her that I would probably fall in love with her. She told me that she had never been kissed before and I said that didn't matter because I would help her and not hurt her.

'I passed all my A levels last Christmas,' I lied to Avril. 'This is just a holiday job to earn some money before I go to Birmingham University. I'm going to study economics.' I kissed her again and tried to feel her small breasts but she pushed me away and said that I was obviously used to easy girls.

After I had taken her back to the Miramar at ten o'clock sharp, as demanded by the harbour-master, whose boats, Avril said, always left and came in on time, I went to a bar and got very drunk. A really pretty, if rather young girl had told me that she thought I had already scaled the highest sexual peaks.

As the cognac and smoke burnt my throat I felt, for the first time, that I was taking long strides towards a place called manhood and doing it without the help of Union Movement, a speaker's platform in Praed Street, Sir Oswald Mosley or, and maybe the most ominous of all, my mother back at 40 Blandford Square.

At the end of her first holiday abroad, Avril leant out of the train window on Port Bou Station and held her hands out to me. Captain Hardy had his eyes on his wristwatch and let the scene pass for what it was, a sweet teenage moment which would never be wiped from my memory. We promised to write to each other.

'I'll visit you in September before I go to university,' I promised, hating myself for lying when she was so lovely. 'We'll go for long walks along the Kentish coast and I can help you with your English literature.'

The train pulled away, watched by stern-looking policemen who, I later learnt, were mainly interested in finding out where the English girls were staying. English girls were regarded in Spain as the easiest girls in Europe.

A few days after Avril's departure I was told by one of the Spanish guides who worked in Port Bou about a brothel in nearby Figueras. During the spring and summer months Spanish men would go with the tourists from Britain, Sweden, Norway and Germany. In winter they made do with whores. Nearly all the young Spaniards had good Catholic girlfriends who were watched over by Catalonian versions of Captain and Mrs Hardy. I never used the brothel. I hadn't the nerve to go there.

Virginity was with me like a disease, but being a courier it was assumed by Spanish men that I at least went to bed with the English girls. 'Some of them do it standing up in the train with men they have just met,' said a guide from Barcelona. 'When they get back to England they are met at Victoria Station and they say, "Hello Mummy, hello Daddy, I've had a really good time learning Spanish and watching the bullfights." Then we get these love letters until the new season and the girl runs up to you at the station and you can't remember her name.' He pulled his mouth down like a bullfighter.

I started practising this macho grimace in the hotel mirror and noticed that I had a bit of a suntan that was camouflaging some of the more unsightly spots which were starting to disappear after only a few weeks away from Blandford Square.

After two weeks in Port Bou, I was ordered from London to go by train to Barcelona and stay there until the end of the season, which was supposed to be the end of September, though there could be trips during the first fortnight of October if the weather and the mistral held. I left the Miramar, said goodbye to my handful of Spanish acquaintances, who told me I should put on weight and have fun with the English girls, and took my suitcase full of books and my steel-stringed guitar to Barcelona.

As soon as I checked in, the concierge handed me a telegram. It was signed by Sid Proud and read: 'Crisis in office. Return by next train.

Bring bank receipt urgentest. Proud – Spanish Travel.'

The hotel manager saw my face and asked what was wrong. I tried to explain to him that I had brought everything with me to Spain, all my books so that I could study as well as work and that I had been promised a room at the hotel until September.

'But the office said that you were to stay only one night, tonight, and the room was booked for you weeks ago.'

He gave me a bottle of wine and I ate a salad and a beef steak on my own. As I entered a world of despair, my dreams of freedom crashing all around me, I looked down and saw a human face close to the floor, moving quite quickly but grimacing at times. The man must have been in his fifties, perhaps his sixties. He had leather pads on his elbows and knees. The manager told me that he had been blown up in the war. 'Not the Second World War, no. Our war, the Spanish War.'

'Was he blown up by the Communists?' I asked, remembering the Spanish Civil War books which my father had kept next to *The Alternative*.

'No. Not the Communists. The Fascists.' The manager looked around the room and moved his head from right to left to see who was nearby and might be listening. 'The Fascists, Franco's soldiers. Some say it wasn't a landmine. Some say he was tortured and that they took off his legs and arms as a punishment. Him? He will not say. He has to live, somehow.'

The following night I took the train back to Port Bou and from there to Paris, where I managed a quick meeting with André at Gare Saint Lazare.

'Beware, my young friend,' he said over a coffee and cognac. 'You are in bed with a monster. You are swimming with a shark. You should still be at school. How old are you? Seventeen? Eighteen? What are you doing working for a man like Proud? Me? It doesn't matter. I work for six other people, that's my job, that's the way I am. But you, you cannot speak French or a word of Spanish and you are a courier?

'It is well-known in travel circles that this man Proud is a crook, a

Fascist crook. He smuggles money into Spain to pay his bills at favourable rates and that means he never transfers British money into a Spanish bank, which is illegal. If he asks you to carry money for him say no and leave, otherwise, my young friend, you are going to end up in a deep, deep puddle.

'Shall I tell you what your life is going to be like if you stay with Proud? He will use you like a dogsbody and you will be bringing British tourists to Spain every week once you have learnt the ropes. He will wear you out and you will be half dead by the end of this season. And what will happen then? I'll tell you. He will throw you onto the rubbish dump. Don't carry money for him. People know who he is and what he's like. Do you know that he pretends to be a big fan of Franco? Ask him why he never dares cross into Spain? Ask him why he never goes to Port Bou? He is a crook and his people bribe crooked Fascists in Barcelona and Madrid but he, he never takes a single risk but lets people like you do his dirty work.'

Before I left for the train to the French coast, André touched my arm. 'Proud is a British Fascist but he really should be an international anarchist. He is one of those men who walk the earth blowing up everything and everyone they touch. The Fascists and the Nazis are dogs and you are too young to know anything about them. But beware of sleeping with monsters and swimming with sharks.'

I returned to 40 Blandford Square with the regulation customs allowance of wine, whisky and cigarettes, which I gave to my mother. She could see that I was deeply disappointed at having had to return early. Mr Proud had telephoned her, she said. 'It's just a temporary crisis,' he'd explained. 'Trevor should come into the office first thing tomorrow. Oh, and tell him not to forget to bring in the bank receipt.'

The following morning I was in the Coventry Street office of Spanish Travel at nine o'clock. Sid Proud was waiting for me.

'Where's the receipt for the money you were supposed to have banked?' Proud snapped without even saying 'hello' or asking how I was. I looked at his manic face and felt suddenly frightened. Timothy Adams, who had been expelled from Haberdashers Askes, and Joe Warren, an ex-Mosleyite from the East End who'd been a champion

161

boxer in the Royal Navy, appeared from the back office. Timothy managed a curt, 'Hello, Trev.'

I fumbled nervously in my wallet and produced a receipt from the Bank of Spain, Port Bou branch. A look of great relief crossed Proud's cracked and ravaged face.

'Oh, so there it is! Now that's well done. So, Trev, you managed all right, did you? Now that's wonderful. I think to celebrate we'll all go and have lunch later on at the Creole, round the corner. Now you go off and have some coffee or do whatever you like for a couple of hours and then we'll have a nice little chat about what I've got planned for you.'

Timothy came across to the coffee shop with me and I asked him if he was working for Spanish Travel.'

'I'm working for Mr Proud – twenty-five pounds a week and all expenses. That's more than my father earns. I've met some really tough people thanks to Sid Proud.'

As he was speaking, sipping coffee and smoking, I realised I'd done Timothy a terrible disservice in introducing him to Union Movement. So many people associated with it, I said to myself, are now birds with broken wings. But were their wings broken before or after they'd encountered Oswald Mosley?

'And the Movement. Do you have anything to do with the Movement?' I asked.

'Fuck Mosley,' he said. 'And fuck his son, Alexander. If you see him, tell him that Mr Proud would like a word or two with him and if he's not inclined to come to Mr Proud, then Mr Proud will be forced to come to him.'

'Tim,' I said, still unconvinced that our Robin Hood/Little John relationship had irrevocably ended, 'you sound like some hoodlum in the "B" movies we used to watch at the Odeon in Edgware Road. What on earth's wrong with you, and what has Alexander done? He's a great guy. You used to like him.'

'I'd stay well away from Mr Alexander Mosley if I were you,' Tim replied cryptically.

At eleven o'clock I went to see Sid Proud, who told me that because of staff shortages and financial problems, which would end about the middle of June, he would need me in the office every Thursday and Friday. That meant me leaving London with the tourists on a Sunday morning from Victoria Station, travelling to Paris and then going all night by train down to Port Bou. After I had banked 'the money' I would have the whole day off 'completely free to do what you want, Trev, chase the girls, have a few drinks'. I would stay the night in the Miramar and leave for Britain on Tuesday, arriving back in London on Wednesday. My salary would stay the same, ten pounds a week, but from June onwards I would be able to sell couchettes between Paris and Port Bou and make extra money.

'From next weekend, Trevor, you'll have two Gladstone bags to take to Port Bou every week, okay? Oh, and never lose the receipts, Trev. We don't want to waste any time or money sending Tim or Joe down to help you find them in Port Bou, now, do we?' And he added, 'And I think you'll have to do all your studying when the season is over. But by then you'll have made so much money you'll be able to do all that reading about William Wordsworth in the Canary Islands or wherever you like, won't you?'

While I'd been in Spain, my mother had taken another telephone call for me. 'Derek's mother rang and asked whether you could ring her. Derek's been taken ill. I told her you'd gone to live in Spain and she said then it didn't matter and that she wouldn't tell Derek in case it made his depression worse.'

I went to visit Derek and received the same sort of reception from his mother as I'd received from Mrs Smith. 'I blame you partly. Not totally, mind you, but partly, because our Derek has always had this strange thing, a sort of worship of Adolf Hitler, even before he got involved with Union Movement. But you people made it worse. You made it worse because you made it acceptable. That's what you did, you made it acceptable instead of something that should have been treated as dangerous. His father hasn't spoken to him for years and why should he? His father lost his eyesight and a leg in the war. It's a good job he can't see what's on Derek's wall, that's what I say.'

Derek was in bed. 'You've come at last, Trevor.' He had an idiotic look on his face but then he'd often worn a disconcerting and distant half-smile. 'Trevor,' he repeated. 'Do you know that's the first time I've said your name in six months?'

I sat on the edge of his bed and looked at the pictures of Hitler on his wall. There were also two or three of Mussolini, a half-dozen of Rudolf Hess and one of me speaking at Trafalgar Square. I felt ill. Examining it, I saw that Derek was behind me, proudly holding the flash-and-circle flag. On his face there was the same slightly inane grin that he was wearing now.

Derek told me how Jeffrey Hamm had expelled him from Union Movement and he had joined one of the Nazi fringe movements. 'But they don't see the Führer the same way I do,' he said. 'The Führer was God, much more than Jesus Christ. Jesus was a Jew, anyhow, so how could he be the same God that the Führer represented, the God of our fathers?'

I told Derek that I was working in Spain and I would come and see him again when I had finished and that he had to look after himself. He had no job, no girlfriend, no political organisation and the words of his mother burnt into my heart: I had allowed Derek to believe that his isolation, his essential oddness, his worship of Hitler were acceptable. I was, I berated myself, partly to blame for the lonely, depressed situation in which he now found himself. I remembered Les Smith lying in bed, beaten to pulp by a collection of Union Movement members. Who was responsible for that? Perhaps I was. I wondered if Mosley ever blamed himself for encouraging unacceptable behaviour in *his* followers. He always seemed to be blessing us, sanctifying our deeds, trying to turn our tiny movement of social oddities into a sort of church. He made constant references to the Spirit, the torch that would light up the world and had said that the black shirt was 'an outward and visible sign of an inward and spiritual grace'. Did he know what he was saying or was it a game to him? He never gave the impression that he felt responsible for us, yet I felt sick with guilt as I sat with my loyal follower, Derek.

Derek stared at me with his strange, dangerous smile, his fine brown hair combed across one side of his forehead like that of the German he loved so much. 'Trevor! They've got you as well, haven't they? The Jews have got you as well as Mosley. Franco was Jewish, you know. Franco is a Jewish name. He refused to support the Führer and closed the Mediterranean to Churchill, and the Führer said that he'd sooner have all his teeth taken out than meet Franco again. And now you're working for him, Trevor. The Jews have got you, as well.'

I returned to Spain, banked Proud's bags of money, chased no girls, consumed a great deal of brandy and many cigarettes and returned to Spanish Travel to repeat the journey week after week for five and a half months. One of the highlights of my week, on a Sunday night, was to sit down at a station café and enjoy a meal with André, whom I liked more and more, even though he was so much older than me.

Our friendship was tested by Proud encouraging me to take over the sale of couchettes during the overnight journey between Paris and Port Bou. That was André's territory and when I told him about the plan he said yes, I could do that but then he would never be my friend again. So I stayed on ten pounds a week.

I told André a little about my strange upbringing and the influence of Oswald Mosley on my life. He said that he had never connected English people with Nazis or Fascists, though he had heard of Mosley. 'We let him live in France which shows how tolerant, or stupid, we are.

'Finish this contract with Proud,' André advised me. 'Save as much as you can and get away from your parents and everyone you know in the Mosley movement. If you want, come to Paris. My wife and I can find some room for you and you can learn French. Get away from that terrible world. If you don't come to France, why don't you keep a month's supply of all that money and run away with it to Morocco. Then disappear. If a man with money sets his mind on disappearing in Africa, no one will ever be able to find him again.'

The idea of stealing a month's supply of Sid Proud's money was appealing but I knew I would be chased around North Africa by people like Joe Warren. But perhaps with such a lot of money in my pocket I could afford to hire my own Joe Warren, an Arab Joe Warren with a sword, I dreamed.

When I asked André about the Germans, he told me that when they occupied Paris they didn't destroy it because Hitler thought it was a magnificent city and wanted to demonstrate to West Europeans, especially the British ruling classes, that he wasn't a monster. 'He showed no such qualms about destruction in Eastern Europe and the Soviet Union.' And for the first time I was able to listen to this without walking out or running away.

During 1958, a year of civil strife throughout France and especially in Paris where the government put tanks on the streets, André supplied me with left-wing magazines and also books in English about the Second World War. I was learning to read French with enthusiasm and starting to pick up a little bit of Spanish.

During these months, I had next to nothing to do with Union Movement. I saw Alexander only two or three times. He looked increasingly sad now that he had found God, broken with Cynthia Proud and Sid had declared some sort of vendetta against the Mosley family. It was impossible to mention The Leader's name in Proud's presence without releasing a diatribe about Mosley being Jewish, his first wife being Jewish and Jeffrey Hamm being a Pope's nark.

Proud was also under financial pressure as the influence he had once exerted on Fascist bureaucrats in Barcelona and Madrid was on the wane. Other large, respectable British travel companies had established themselves there and Spanish Travel was seen as a cheapskate organisation which couldn't keep up with the changing requirements of holiday-makers as the 1960s approached. People no longer wanted twenty-pound holidays to Port Bou. They were looking further south, to Valencia and more exciting parts of the Costa Brava.

One Wednesday evening, returning from France, I opened the kitchen door and failed to receive the normal, excited welcome from my mother. I unloaded a carrier bag and put a carton of duty free cigarettes and a bottle of sherry onto the table.

'There you are, Mum. Some for you and some for me.' It was the standard joke, but no laughter was heard.

She looked at me, her large, dark eyes full of pain. 'I'm going to tell you something that will break your heart.'

'God,' I thought, 'what new piece of drama?'

'Derek's dead.' She put her arms around me and almost whispered. 'After you'd gone to see him, he told his mother he felt better. The following week he left home with some shirts and socks and not much else in a case. On Monday, the police went round to the house and told his mother that Derek had been found . . . drowned in the Rhine, near Munich. They said it was an accident. His mother told Jeffrey. She didn't shout or anything. She just told him the few facts and put the phone down.'

I screwed the top off the sherry bottle and poured my mother a glass. I knocked back the sweet, sickly drink and then had another and another. Derek had told me more than once that one day he wanted to visit the place on the Rhine where the ashes of the twelve Nazi leaders executed at Nuremberg had been unceremoniously dumped.

I pictured his small body floating on the waters of the great German river and there was a smile on his cold, white face. I remembered his mother's chilling words, 'You people made it worse . . . You made it worse because you made it acceptable' and thought my heart would break.

Whether Jeffrey Hamm told The Leader about Derek, and the effect his death had had on me, I shall never know. But shortly after the suicide of this strange, lonely Welsh boy I received a phone call from Hamm. He said that Sir Oswald and Lady Mosley had invited me to supper when I was next in Paris, and that I should ring to say when I would be coming. Despite the fact that I'd been feeling disillusioned with the Movement, with my role in it and even with Mosley, when The Leader smiled down on me again, my heart leapt.

I took the metro from central Paris to Orsay, where Sir Oswald's loyal retainer, Jerry, picked me up.

At Le Temple de la Gloire, having made sure that I had a drink, Sir Oswald Mosley went to his desk and returned with a glossy white booklet written by him, entitled *Wagner and Shaw*. On it he had written in red pen: 'For Trevor Grundy who has done so much for our movement.' He signed it and handed it to me.

At the dinner table, I thought Mosley was charming, though I later realised that he talked to me in the way he did to all children. Lady Mosley rolled her eyes. She looked bored and said next to nothing. Alexander and Max were there. Max, who had just been told he had a place at Oxford, spent a great deal of time talking about Elvis Presley, and how he would be the Prime Minister of Britain if he were British. Mosley seemed to enjoy this banter and Max delighted his mother by doing yet another imitation of Elvis. He performed on the balcony and I looked out across the green lawn and saw a swan. Shouldn't the music have been from *Parsifal* rather than 'Jailhouse Rock'?

Briefly, I sat down next to Lady Mosley and told her that the previous winter had been extremely cold but that hadn't stopped the winter campaign being successful and The Leader magnificent.

'At the height of winter the local shops took advantage of the cold to put up the price of paraffin and make it more expensive for people to run oil heaters,' I informed The Leader's wife.

She looked at me with large, beautiful, almost cow-like eyes and said, 'What *is* an oil heater?'

Mosley flashed his eyes at me. 'And what are you going to do when you stop working in Spain?' he asked.

'I plan to take my A levels and try to get into university by the end of next year, sir.'

'You don't still feel destined for the Church, then?'

'I'm no longer sure. I think I'll wait until you get into power before doing something like that, sir.'

I told him that while in Spain I had met a reporter from the *Newcastle Journal* who'd told me that, if I liked writing and knew a bit about the north-east, an area where I'd spent many sun-filled holidays, I should apply to the paper for a job as a junior reporter. I'd decided that the job would admirably fill in the year before university and had written to the editor. 'But perhaps I'll like journalism so much that I won't want to go to university . . . Fleet Street's dominated by Jews but the provinces are probably much better.'

Mosley agreed. 'I have always known what you say to be true, Grundy.' He called everyone other than his social peers by their surnames, military style.

I dread to think what he must have said when I left, but Mosley on the balcony outside Paris on that August evening returned me to an earlier state of awareness and development. He had been my life and, despite the efforts of Father Crisp and André Négar, still was.

On the metro back to Paris I read the inscription on the booklet perhaps a hundred times. The first sentence of his book read: 'The man of action in the realm of art is a helpless being.' I would always remember that, along with Lady Mosley's naïve question about normal life in a Britain which her husband still hoped to lead.

9

As I walked towards Port Bou Station for the last time, an American newspaper caught my eye. RACE RIOTS BREAK OUT IN NOTTING HILL GATE, screamed the headline. My heart thudding, I bought the paper, turned to the nearest bar, ordered a large cognac and lit a cigarette. Full of dread, I read the article.

London, September 9 – *Race riots flared in Britain last night. Petrol bombs and thousands of milk bottles were thrown at police in West London after white youths taunted black immigrants with racist slogans. Rioting continued throughout much of the night and this morning the streets of Notting Hill Gate are strewn with broken glass and debris.*

Several people were badly injured when a group of white youths began demonstrating outside a house occupied by black people in Blenheim Crescent. They were met by a hail of milk bottles and a petrol bomb, which exploded on the pavement.

Within minutes, black men had begun a counter-attack with iron bars. Although police broke this incident up and dispersed both mobs, sporadic fighting continued, with police advising black people to stay at home.

A black and his girlfriend were chased down Lancaster Road by a white mob shouting, 'Let's get the blacks' and in Bayswater black men were ambushed as they left a club in Ledbury Road. Three petrol bombs were thrown.

Special Branch is investigating the possibility of extreme right-wing movements behind the rioting.

.

I felt sick. I returned to the Miramar just half an hour before the departure of the train to Paris, asked for a typewriter and, as fast as I could, wrote an airmail letter to the editor of the *Newcastle Journal*.

I told him that I had received his kind letter offering to interview me in Newcastle at the expense of his newspaper. The editor had written that there was a position as a trainee reporter available, open to someone with acceptable O level qualifications, including English, Pitman's shorthand and a good knowledge of north-east England. If suitable, I would be able to start immediately.

'I will telephone you the moment I return to London,' I wrote. I stuck a stamp on the envelope and slipped it into the hotel delivery tray, wondering how long it would take me to learn shorthand.

I said goodbye again to the hotel manager, who told me in broken English that I needed to rest, put on weight and change my diet. He touched his face and then pointed at mine. The waiter translated. 'He says you look terrible.'

I picked up my bag and my guitar, which I had still not learnt to play, and looked at myself in the mirror. Sad brown eyes stared back at me. I examined my face and skin. No wonder I was still a virgin.

In Paris, I stayed the night with André and his wife. He told me that French radio broadcasts were saying that Oswald Mosley was behind the Notting Hill Gate race riots, but a spokesman for Mosley had strongly denied that he had anything to do with the riots and asserted that Mosley wasn't in England when they broke out.

'What are you going to do, Trevor? Keep away.'

I told him about the possibility of a job offer at the other end of England, a place called Newcastle. 'Either that, or I'll come here.'

André must have seen plenty of worried young men on the run. 'Be careful you don't get pulled back, sucked in,' he warned.

The train from the English coast arrived at Victoria Station shortly after six o'clock. I was tired with a weariness I had never known before, a soul weariness. I wanted to be with Lovene, who was pregnant, and with my mother. The following day I would go to see Sid Proud, sort out any office problems and leave. The season was coming to an end and the last few trips to Spain were being done by someone else. Maybe I would see Alexander.

'Hello, old man.' John was waiting at the ticket collection gate with three or four Union Movement members, including James. 'Welcome home. My dear boy, we're going to need your dulcet tones. Have you heard the news? The whole of Notting Hill Gate is up in arms. I tell you, Trev, it's going to be as big as the East End, perhaps bigger.'

I wanted to run.

They jostled around me, one of them helping me with my case, which was quite heavy.

'Jeffrey Hamm's called a meeting of London branch leaders tonight at 302, Trev,' John said. 'He specifically requested that you be there. We're going to need you to speak in Notting Hill Gate.'

Vauxhall Bridge Road was across the road from Victoria Station, so instead of going home we went to the Shakespeare pub nearby.

'I'm really tired,' I said to John, weakly trying to excuse myself. The remark was ignored.

'Jeffrey says that the Old Man has been kept in the picture and will be coming across from France,' said James, revelling in the excitement. 'The whole place is seething and the Teds are one hundred per cent behind us. They were shouting Mosley slogans all over the place and the Old Man is a local hero. You won't believe what's happening, Trev! It's like a dream come true and I don't think even the Old Man knew anything about it. I mean, it just sort of happened and now everyone's looking to OM to lead them. You'll really be able to take off with the youth league – there are thousands of kids just waiting to be told what to do. I tell you, it could be bigger than the East End before the war.'

I telephoned my mother and covered up my right ear because of the noise.

'You've heard the news? Jeffrey wants to see you immediately.'

'I know. Johnny and James and some of the others are here with me at Victoria Station.'

'So you'll go?'

'Should I?'

'Should you? This is The Leader's greatest opportunity since the war and a son of mine asks, "Should I?" Did St Paul say, "Should I?" when he fell off his donkey?'

I returned to the table.

'Wow,' said Johnny in his public school voice. 'You certainly know how to knock back the brandies, Trev!' He laughed approvingly. 'Spain must have put some hairs on your chest.'

After many drinks, I trundled my way across the road to 302 and joined the rest of the people who had been called together by Jeffrey Hamm in the headquarters' upper room.

A transformation had taken place in Jeffrey Hamm. He was wearing a double-breasted grey suit, a white shirt and silver tie, his hair neatly cut to reveal a prominent widow's peak. The day before, it transpired, a reporter had interviewed him and commented on his dirty shirt and generally grubby appearance. He now looked like a buyer at D.H. Evans in Oxford Street.

We sat down, perhaps as many as forty people crammed into the room. Soon the atmosphere was thick with cigarette smoke.

Jeffrey Hamm gave us the official line: 'Racial problems have been building up in Britain for the last few years. I think all of us in the room tonight know about that. But how did this situation come about? Why did our coloured friends come here? Why didn't they stay in their homes in the West Indies? Well, let me tell you.

'Soon after the last war, when Britain was bankrupt, living off American charity like a whore lives off a client, the Attlee government made a deal with the Americans. "If you let our cars into America so we can earn precious dollars," the British said, "we'll stop buying sugar from the West Indies and buy it, instead, from Cuba, which you control." It was called the Black Pact and later the Conservatives renewed it.

'So, the West Indians couldn't sell their sugar and they started to come here. They said they were British citizens and had every right to live here. And now they're coming here in their thousands, their tens of thousands, along with their friends from India and Pakistan.

'But what happened next, my friends? What happened was this: the

British government gave immigrants enough money – *our* money – to feed themselves and pay their rent. And the crooks, the Jews, our "friends" from long ago, saw an opportunity. They started buying up old houses in places like Birmingham and Notting Hill Gate and started to get rid of white tenants by terrorising them with Alsatian dogs and holding all-night parties. Then they put the immigrants into the rooms, a dozen at a time and charged each immigrant rent. Rent paid for by you and me, paid for by the British tax-payers. The practice of driving British people out of British homes is one of the most monstrous things ever done in this country!' he roared. Jeffrey and his audience were warming to the subject.

'The old men of the old parties have sat back and watched a crisis develop without moving as much as a finger. While they live in Hampstead, Highgate, the Cotswolds and Bournemouth, ordinary working-class white Britons are forced to live next to people who are used to an entirely different way of life . . . carnivals in the street, music all hours of the day and night . . . free sex, and lots of it . . .

'The same people who pushed us into a disastrous war against Germany are now pushing the British people to the edge of a new cliff. They're saying to us, "*You* move, if you don't like it. *You* go live elsewhere. Our *new friends*, the *blacks* from the Commonwealth, are much more important to us than you *white* people who've lived here all your lives.'

In the room, members started to clap and cheer.

'The smoked salmon socialists and the cocktail circuit revolutionaries are at it again, telling working people what to do and how to live, while they go off on holiday to the Bahamas and Bermuda.'

He drew a deep breath. 'So what's the answer? The answer is to start buying West Indian sugar once again and then say to the immigrants, "Look, my friends, you have beautiful warm islands with clear blue skies and warm, warm seas where you can swim. You have wonderful golden beaches. Go back and dance on them, not on our staircases at night."'

There were roars of laughter. I smiled, then laughed with the others. When the mirth had died down, Jeffrey looked us in the eye and spoke soberly.

'Next year, there'll be a general election. We must persuade ordinary people in Notting Hill Gate to vote for The Leader. We must show them how they've been done over once more by the old men of the old parties. There are thousands of young people out there – the Teddy Boys – who will flock to the flash and circle and the Union Jack once they hear The Leader. Mosley will put across his policy not just on immigration but on "Europe a Nation – Africa the Empire".

'It will be bigger than the East End. Bigger than anything any of us have seen before in Britain. And if we're prepared to dedicate ourselves in a way that we've never dedicated ourselves before, we'll win and in that mighty process we'll win back the soul of Britain.'

Jeffrey's policy statement was greeted by a tumultuous round of applause. The fire had descended and was blazing on our heads. We were a band of brothers and I found a dozen or so hardened old East-Enders slapping me on the back and asking where I had been, and was I all right because I looked ill. Jeffrey Hamm took me to one side and said that The Leader had great hopes that I could play a meaningful role telling people about the Movement's sensible policies. Mosley would finance a new newspaper for Notting Hill Gate called the *North Kensington Leader* and I should write for it. Mosley, he said, had been very impressed when he had met me in Paris and he knew that the whole Grundy family would back him one hundred per cent.

John helped me carry my bag and guitar back to Blandford Square. When I got to my room I lay on the bed and tears came to my eyes. I decided to take down all the pictures of Mosley in my room and give them to . . . I originally thought, to Derek. But Derek was dead, so I left them where they were, Hitler staring at Anthony Perkins.

I wanted Avril and I wanted to talk to André. I wanted to be back in the starlit café world of Vincent Van Gogh. 'Don't get caught. Don't get involved again. Don't get sucked in,' André had warned. But without him near me, I felt as if I were bobbing in a rough ocean without a lifebelt.

I woke up the next morning tired and listless. I thought about phoning the editor of the *Newcastle Journal* but couldn't face it. How could I go there, where I didn't know a soul? What was I thinking of? Why would I succeed in the north-east as a journalist when I'd been hopeless at school and remained a penniless virgin in Spain . . . ? Better to stick with what I knew, even if I'd started to hate it. And I could always pretend to myself that I was helping to save the soul of Britain.

Notting Hill Gate gave the sixty-three-year-old Sir Oswald Mosley his final chance to shine. Like Don Quixote, an earlier legend who also found it hard to live in his own century, Mosley turned up in the race-torn London borough on a clapped-out horse with a collection of Sanchos who were prepared to walk, ride or slide with him to the edge of British Fascism's last cliff.

Union Movement set up a second headquarters in Notting Hill Gate and every member was asked to spend time handing out leaflets, selling *Union*, and circulating the free broadsheet, the *North Kensington Leader*. In its first issue I wrote an article which repeated almost word for word what Jeffrey Hamm had told us on the night of my return home from Spain. I ended with words which were often quoted by journalists: 'Most coloured immigrants are decent folk. They are victims of a vicious system which they cannot understand.'

Peter Shaw, who later left Union Movement to help organise the National Front, did not agree. 'Instead of writing moderate articles in a paper which nobody reads, we should get hold of an immigrant and hang him upside-down from Blackfriar's Bridge with a notice round his neck saying "Coloureds go home". That would give us the publicity we need to kick off the campaign and get Mosley elected.'

When this was reported to The Leader, Shaw was called in and reprimanded, but back in Notting Hill Gate he told us, 'Okay, I was bollocksed by the Old Man. He shouted at me and said, "Never do that again, Shaw." Then, God's Truth, he looked at me and he winked.'

Several hundred Teds joined the Notting Hill Gate branch of the Movement. Hundreds of Irish people also supported or joined the

Movement because of Mosley's condemnation of the Black and Tans in the 1920s. There were tens of thousands of Irish living in the area, immigrants to England during another period, under not completely different circumstances from the ones which forced the West Indians to come to England in the 1950s.

Mosley walked to meetings and was followed by his long-time supporters and often hundreds of Teds who thought it was great to hear this aristocratic figure articulating their fouler thoughts about non-whites. West Indians stood and stared as he walked past; most seemed ignorant of who he was, or indifferent.

I had grown my hair quite long and started wearing a duffel coat. One night, one of the Teds guarding Mosley's truck, which had a large platform, microphone and loudspeaker mounted on it so he could tour the area and speak at street corners, looked at me and said something about 'fuckin' lefties'.

'Don't be daft,' said one of the older members. 'He's one of us.'

'Don't look it,' said the Ted and I was quite pleased. I realised that I had nothing in common with the Teds, or the people who were flocking to Mosley not because of his policies on Europe but because he was an upper-class stick with which to beat the blacks.

I told Jeffrey Hamm that I would never speak in Notting Hill Gate.

'You're letting the Movement down badly, Trevor,' he said. 'It'll be remembered when Sir Oswald wins a seat in Parliament and needs writers and speakers to tour Britain with him.'

I often saw Max Mosley and his girlfriend Jean in the Notting Hill Gate area, canvassing, talking to Teds and chatting to reporters, but we no longer spoke. Max was about to go up to Oxford to read physics and now moved in loftier circles. One day I saw a picture of him with Alexander in the *Daily Mirror*. They were dressed in Teddy Boy suits and looked aggressive in an upper-class sort of way.

'We've come down here to help,' Max was quoted as saying. He looked almost pretty and rather like his mother. Alexander was the double of his father during the days when The Leader had worn black and limped into meetings like a wounded giant to cries of 'Mosley! Mosley! Mosley!'

But Alexander also looked sad. Soon after the *Daily Mirror* published his picture, Alexander came to Blandford Square.

'I want to go away from this God-forsaken island. I want to go and live in South America, where things are real and there's a possibility of change and meaning. I need to get away from Dad. The trouble is, I look so much like him . . . And I'm young.' Alexander looked at his hands and his rather short fingers. 'Peasant's hands,' he said. 'Like my Aunt Unity's.' Then he put them round his head and ears as if to shut out noise or pain. 'He laughs because I'm doing weightlifting. He tells everyone that it's the only sport where you compete against yourself.' Alexander turned and looked for a long time at a photograph I had on the wall. It showed Mosley laughing and patting a Swedish fencer on the shoulder after a match. 'My mother's no help. You know she couldn't bear Cynthia. And she thinks that you're a bad influence, too.'

I felt as though he'd stabbed me. 'Me or the family?' I asked, trying to appear nonchalant.

'You.'

'Did she give any reason?'

'Why should she? She rarely does.'

My mother had the habit of knocking on the door and bringing in tea or coffee when Alexander came to the house. She came in now, sat on my bed and stared at him, just as she stared at Mosley in meetings.

'I've something to show you, Alexander,' she said. It was her Christmas card to Sir Oswald and Lady Mosley. She made an enormous fuss about it. 'It cost seven shillings and sixpence.' Alexander looked bored.

'Mrs Grundy. I am tired of Old Members treating my father as if he were Jesus Christ. He's just an ordinary man, you know, an ordinary man with human failings, believe it or not. Do you know what happens every year to those precious Christmas cards from Old Members? Every year our housekeeper in Paris collects them in a large bag and burns them.'

My mother stood up and left the room and I heard the kitchen door close.

I went along the corridor, opened the door and saw my mother sitting staring into space. She was silent and for a few minutes I said nothing to help or comfort her.

'The Leader's Christmas card,' she said, 'is that what happens?'

I put my arms around her. 'Of course not, Mum. Alexander's just a bit fed up. I think he's had a quarrel with his father. He didn't mean it, Mum. Honestly. He didn't mean it, I don't think.'

My mother straightened up and tried a smile. 'Of course not.'

When I returned to my room Alexander had gone. He never came to the house again.

That night I had a vivid dream. In it, Father Crisp appeared in hobnailed boots, a flowing cassock and cardinal's hat. He was wiping egg and tomato from his Friar Tuck face. He told me that he forgave me for throwing things at him but that he could not forgive my mother for muddling Mosley up with God. He said, 'Didn't I say all those years ago that it was a terrible sin and those who worship men must pay a terrible price?' Then I saw rows of marchers with Communist banners turning into Baker Street and disappearing down the wooden steps which led to Lovene's and John's flat in the basement of 40 Blandford Square. I awoke feeling restless and worried.

Though I was no longer comfortable in the heart of the Movement, I didn't know where else to go. I had no friends in London outside Union Movement and no home outside London. So, uncomfortably, I became a sort of fellow traveller and even canvassed quite a lot following Mosley's adoption meeting at the Argyll Hall on 6 April 1959. At that meeting about six hundred people heard Sir Oswald explain the intricacies of his wage-price mechanism to control the respective economies of Europe. He repeated highlights from his great speeches which told of his pre-war attempt to stop Britain's slide into decline and international oblivion but hardly spoke about the coloured invasion and the audience left disappointed.

Mosley gave the appearance of enjoying himself most at street corner meetings. After his main speech, which would leave the Teds shouting for more, he'd offer the platform on his truck to anyone who

179

cared to say anything about life in Notting Hill Gate. Mosley would stand down for housewives who told cheering audiences that the blacks were taking over their streets or that the West Indians were walking around with white girls and playing juke boxes all night to force ordinary English folk out of their flats. Mosley would look terribly concerned and applaud enthusiastically when the extemporary speech was finished.

One night I spotted Colin Wilson in the crowd. Wilson was writing regularly for a Carmelite monthly magazine, the *Aylesford Review*, which was sympathetic towards Mosley. Nicholas Mosley was also there, along with several high-ranking members of the Roman Catholic Church who had been invited to the meeting by Jeffrey Hamm.

Mosley talked about 'Europe a Nation' and how the collective genius of the European could give birth to the greatest civilisation man had ever known. He then took up the immigration issue and it was obvious he was not following the lines drawn up by his secretary, Jeffrey Hamm. He started crouching and behaving as he had done when he'd formed Union Movement in 1948, shouting, ranting and raving that West Indian men captured English girls and kept them locked in a flat where the girls were repeatedly raped.

When he saw the reaction of the audience he repeated several times that he was in Notting Hill Gate to 'call a spade a spade'.

I was looking at the face of Colin Wilson, whom I admired, when Mosley repeated one of the crudest slogans ever used by the Notting Hill Gate Teds. 'As they say, my friends, "Lassie for dogs, Kitty Kat for wogs".' (Lassie was a well-known brand of dog food and Kitty Kat was equally well-known for feeding cats. It was rumoured that poorer immigrants lived on a tin of cat food a day.) Wilson's face reflected the horror he felt. I cringed.

As the election drew nearer, Mosley's confidence grew. One evening, I attended an election tactics meeting.

We were looking at possible photos to use in an advertisement campaign. Mosley shifted some photos on the selection table and spotted one of him about to shake hands with a supporter in Trafalgar

Square, with me standing behind him. 'Nice pair of eyebrows, Grundy,' he joked. In the end he chose one of him walking towards the camera looking like an elderly Clark Gable in *Gone with the Wind*. Over this life-sized black-and-white picture of him was to be printed the new slogan.

'I chose it myself,' he said. 'The new slogan,' he announced, 'is "He is Coming".'

I caught the eye of my brother-in-law. Was it possible? Did he understand what would be scrawled across the posters by the opposition parties?

'I hope "He is Coming" isn't too Biblical . . .' he said.

The following week almost every Mosley poster in Notting Hill Gate showed him with a massive erection. The slogan 'He is Coming' was followed by a large 'whoopee' or 'lucky sod' in red paint.

Several times, I went canvassing with my mother, who was suffering from terrible depressions and mood swings. Once, I asked her what was wrong and she told me that she no longer really believed in Mosley, not in the way she used to. 'I still love him and admire his courage, Trevor, but I think he might be an actor.'

That night in the kitchen she said, 'I'll never be able to see him in the same way, Trevor, not now that I know the Old Members' Christmas cards are burnt.'

'Huh!' snorted my father. 'If Mosley ever comes to power, the first people he'll drop will be the Old Members. We'd be the new opposition,' he said. 'Mosley would be more *national* than *socialist*. He's still a member of White's Club. They all back each other when they're in power. I tell you this, Edna, the *first* and *last* National Socialist was Adolf Hitler.' He looked at my mother and shook his head. 'Mosley? I think we were fooled, Edna. I think we were fooled a long time ago.'

One night, as we were walking along the Portobello Road, my mother said to me, 'I think I made a terrible mistake, Trevor. I think that I muddled Mosley up with Jesus.'

A searing anger burnt through me. I wanted to take her by the shoulders, shake her and scream: 'Yes and what do you think it's been like for me growing up with your obsession?' But I knew there was no point. The next day, she'd be cheerful again, talking about how only Mosley could save the British people and stop the blacks and Jews taking over the country. 'You're not doing enough to help The Leader, Trevor,' she'd say. 'You're not speaking or trying to recruit anyone.'

When I once told her that I regretted parts of my childhood, she looked stunned.

'You know, Mum,' I continued, 'someone once told me that I was the sort of person who'd never believe in anything after the age of thirty.'

'If the blacks take over, you won't reach thirty,' she snapped back and we continued knocking on doors, appealing to people to vote for *Sir* Oswald Mosley and his Union Movement.

Another evening, when she was down again, she let me into her past for the first time. The door which led to her childhood and youth opened, but only for a moment.

'I had a terrible childhood, Trevor. I know your father and I row, but he's been my salvation. He rescued me from a terrible fate in London when I was young. My parents used me . . .' she trailed off into silence and stood still in the street.

I wanted to say, 'But I *know*, Mummy, I know. Daddy told me that awful night when you and Lovene went to stay at the rector's . . .'

When she was in high spirits again, she'd talk about the Jews and what they'd done to Mosley. 'The Jews forced the BBC to ban his voice. The Jews run everything, Trevor.'

'But you,' I joked, 'you look like a right old four-by-two yourself, Mum. You could easily pass as a Jewess, if you wanted to.'

She looked pleased. 'Do you think so? It's my mother's nose and eyes. We might have Spanish blood.' Then she said again, 'Jewish? Do you think so? Well, that would make you a Jew, wouldn't it, because our line is matriarchal.'

I stopped dead in the street. '*Our* line, Mum? What on earth do you mean, *our* line?'

She was brilliant at changing the subject and never replied. It was too bizarre even to start thinking about, but one night as we canvassed in Notting Hill Gate I was forced to think again.

My mother had knocked on a door in a large housing block and the man who answered looked at her and smiled broadly. He was registered as Mr Harold Lewin.

'Mr Lewin.' She smiled back. 'Mr Lewin, we're representing Union Movement, *Sir* Oswald Mosley's party, and we'd like to talk to you about the coming election. We believe that a vote for Oswald Mosley will be a vote for the British people in Parliament and, even though you might have heard a lot of nonsense about Mosley in the past, we'd like to invite you to his next meeting which will be at . . .'

Mr Lewin was smoking. He dogged his cigarette with his foot.

'Come on,' he said, still smiling. 'Who are you trying to kid? Who put you up to this?' He started to laugh. 'Larry did, didn't he? Larry. Silly sod that he is, Larry. What is it? Some sort of birthday joke? Now, when is my birthday? It's a joke, isn't it? I mean, you're not being *serious* are you? Are you one of Larry's relatives or . . .'

We left Mr Lewin standing in his doorway, still confused, as we eased our way down the corridor towards the stairs from the flats and into the street. My mother was almost crying with laughter.

'He thinks I'm a Jewess,' she said. 'He really thinks I'm a Jewess. I must tell your father. He was convinced I'm a Jewess, wasn't he, Trevor? Convinced. I must tell your father.'

I had often felt nervous and uncomfortable in my parents' company when they'd started drumming on about race and the Jews but, as we walked away from Mr Lewin's flats towards Mosley's headquarters in Notting Hill Gate where we would report our night's canvassing efforts, I felt not only spiritually exhausted but physically sick.

When we got home that night she told my father about the night's canvassing and how most of the people we'd met had said that they'd sooner have the West Indians in Notting Hill Gate than Mosley representing them in Parliament. Maybe one in ten had said they'd vote for him or thought he was right about immigration. Mostly, people were indifferent or indicated they'd never heard of Mosley.

Back at the Notting Hill Gate headquarters, other canvassers had reported to Mosley and Jeffrey Hamm that everyone they spoke to was screaming for The Leader and that it would be a hands-down win. The sturdy, almost hefty, Mosley seemed to grow in stature and started to behave as if he were already Prime Minister of Britain. He repeated his old rallying cry: If he could win thirty or thirty-five per cent of the vote in Notting Hill Gate, he would be able to sweep the country. Only a few years before he came to power, Hitler had had far less support in Germany. We listened and nodded our agreement, and more and more supporters came through the door with ticks in the 'definitely' column of their canvass sheets.

My father was still driving his cab most hours of the day and night but one evening he came down to Notting Hill Gate and joined a group of supporters at one of the local pubs, one which didn't mind hosting 'the Mosley boys', who were quite big spenders when it came to booze.

'Haven't seen you in a while, Sid.'

In a loud, provocative voice, my father said that Mosley was trying to repeat his days of glory in the East End of London but that he'd never win in Notting Hill Gate. 'People are too comfortable. It's what Macmillan said: "Never had it so good." Ordinary people don't want Mosley because they can't see any problems and all he'll do here is work people up and then they'll vote Labour. Mosley is wasting his time and should pack it in.'

I thought there might be a fight. But there was just a bitter argument, which I left my father to. I noticed a couple of obvious outsiders sitting together at a table, exchanging notes. Probably Special Branch, I thought, a typically paranoid Union Movement reaction to anything out of the ordinary. One was wearing a full-length brown leather coat. He had a thin, unusual, aristocratic face with brown hair and a large nose. He stood up when the pub door opened and in a voice which revealed his background and education said, 'Jeffrey! My *dear* Jeffrey! What *would* you like to drink? *Blissful* beer or *dreamy* gin? You must be *exhausted* after coming so *heroically* out of the trenches.'

Jeffrey Hamm stood and spoke to the man and his companion for about ten minutes.

'Who on earth is that?' I asked Freddie Shepherd.

'That's Alan Neame. He's a writer friend of Lady Mosley. Writes for the *European* on poetry. Family owns a brewery down in Kent.'

The writer must have known we were talking about him because he looked up and gave us a knowing stare. Minutes later, he was at the bar talking to my father about his days in prison and what he thought Mosley would achieve, or otherwise, in Notting Hill Gate. I heard him say that he was writing an article for *The Tablet*, the well-known Roman Catholic magazine.

Later he turned to me and said, 'Your father is quite wonderful. He seems to think that The Leader is copping out, taking on the blacks and not the Jews. I rather agree. My goodness, at least the Jews were a reputable enemy. I can't say that for most of the poor dears walking around here with banjos and bananas. I feel rather sorry for them, don't you? I mean coming from their lovely island in the sun to Latimer Road.'

Alan asked me to join him for supper the following week at a restaurant in the Edgware Road. I said I would. 'Sidney is wonderful,' said Alan as he tightened his belt around a coat which made him look like an SS intelligence officer, 'but I don't think we need to invite him next week, do you?'

A group of Freddie Shepherd's boys came and spoke to me after the poet and his friend had left the bar. Freddie said, 'Watch it, Trev. Did I hear him ask you out?'

'Why not? I'd love to talk to Alan Neame, especially about poetry.'

'Poetry, my arse,' replied Freddie, as he gathered up his entourage to leave for another bar.

A former member, whom I knew only as Tony, decided for some reason that he should also warn me off Alan Neame. 'Be careful,' he said, 'people like him just use you. He's well-known as one of Lady Mosley's entertainers. She surrounds herself with people like that. They all go across to have meetings about the *European* and they always turn into parties. They're not serious. I've seen Jeffrey and Bob Row desperate for their regular pay cheques, while Alan Neame and Desmond Stewart waltz into 302 to collect their waiting payment cheques for articles in the *European*. Once, Jeffrey was called across to Paris to see Mosley about something or other, a new book, I think, and Jeff hadn't eaten for a couple of days. When the servant brought Jeffrey a sandwich, Mosley grabbed it from his mouth, ordered him to take some dictation, and then told him to get straight back to London. They spend a fortune entertaining the Mitford sisters and I'm sure a couple of meals with wine cost the Old Man as much as Jeffrey's annual salary. Mosley calls the Mitford women "the sillies" and Alan Neame is part of that set, him and Desmond Stewart. They're clever, I admit that. Brilliant, in fact. But what does he want with you, Trev?'

At the height of the Notting Hill Gate election campaign Oswald Mosley telephoned 40 Blandford Square and asked to speak to me. My mother told me when I returned from National Cash, where I had taken an undemanding clerking job in order to give me time to study for my A levels. I thought she had St Vitus's Dance. Despite her new-found scepticism about The Leader she still, quite clearly, adored him. And I was no better. In a state of excitement, I rang The Leader at his London house in Cheyne Walk.

'Grundy, if you have time, it would be appreciated. It's a personal matter.'

I went by Underground to Sloane Square and walked the rest of the way. I looked around and wondered if Cheyne Walk and Notting Hill Gate were on the same planet. I passed large, expensive cars outside magnificent homes whose walls were decorated with blue plaques commemorating the lives of famous people.

Jerry, Sir Oswald's manservant, let me in, regarding me with the mixture of snobbery and self-assurance which long-standing servants of the aristocracy acquire. 'Sir Oswald is expecting you upstairs, Mr Grundy,' he said in his Irish lilt.

Mosley was wearing a herring-bone jacket and open-necked shirt. He'd been writing at his desk and looked extremely tired. He came quickly to the point.

He knew that I was a friend of his son, Alexander, and that I had also been working for Sid Proud. He was concerned that Proud would publish a pamphlet accusing Mosley of encouraging Alexander to dodge his National Service. National Service had ended for those born after the first quarter of 1940, but Alexander had been born in 1938. He had been brought up in Ireland, but an accusation that Alexander was not going to do his patriotic duty would have done enormous damage to Mosley during the build-up to the 1959 election. Mosley asked me to go to see Sid Proud to find out what he wanted to stop the flow of bad blood between the two men who had once been 'comrades'.

It was a massive honour. I was to be a 'discreet ambassador' on behalf of The Leader! I promised I'd do my best and report back to him immediately.

The following day I telephoned and asked Proud if I could meet him at his Coventry Street office. When I arrived, he was with Joe Warren and a tall, menacing-looking man with a moustache. I passed on Mosley's message, nervous in front of the two yobs who no doubt wanted to give me a good thumping to justify their week's wages.

'So now you're a Mosley nark, are you? First a Jesus nark, now a Mosley nark,' Proud snarled at me. 'Tell your Leader that his son has treated my daughter like *scum*. Tell him that. Like *dirt*. Tell him the pamphlet is going under every door in Notting Hill Gate tomorrow bloody morning. Tell him that, and you can bugger off as fast as you came, Mosley nark.'

I returned to Cheyne Walk and repeated what Proud had said. I dared to add that Proud was a disgusting little man and that it was horrible to see a man like Mosley have to ask him for any kind of favour. Mosley looked at me, almost with contempt, and waved his hand in my direction, saying, 'Enough of that.'

I had failed him.

He waved his arm towards the door, dismissing me. As I left the room, I heard him shout downstairs to Jerry, 'Get me Lane.' Lane was his solicitor. The pamphlets were never circulated and not long after I heard that Alexander had left for Latin America.

As I trod a weary path back to Marylebone Station, I thought, 'I've really let him down.' But then I thought, 'But why am I being used like this? Why am I spending time running between Cheyne Walk and Coventry Street to make a bridge for two men old enough to be my grandparents? Why?'

That night I met Alan Neame at an Italian restaurant on Edgware Road. I told him that I was a speaker for the Movement and his eyes widened as he poured oil and vinegar into a large spoon to make a salad dressing, something that seemed so clever and different at the time.

'My dear boy,' said Alan, 'surely it's time that you thought about *yourself* and stopped whizzing around like a firework for *The Leader* and his family. Mosley has plenty of lawyers if he wants to take on the demonic Mr Proud, who sounds quite awful. When all this Notting Hill Gate thing is over, the precious Leader will take off for Venice, or wherever, and you'll be left wondering what to do next with three O levels, slaving away for the cash register company. Surely that's not what a good National Socialist boy such as yourself wants.'

It was hard to know whether Alan was being serious. He made me laugh so much I could hardly eat. Most of his jokes involved The Leader, the Mitford 'sillies' and the poor Movement members who thought their salvation would come from supporting such people. Yet where did that leave Alan, if he was one of them? Did people like Alan spend their lives turning gossip into art and writing amusing poems about their friends? He seemed to think everything was one big joke.

At the end of the meal, Alan said that he was writing a book about a woman guerrilla leader in Africa, called Maud, and that some of the Union Movement people might appear in it, heavily disguised.

He said that he would like to see me again and bring round some books on English literature which might interest me. If he found time, he might even tutor me a little, he said, but only if I stopped reading books about Jews and Adolf Hitler's Germany.

Weeks later, when Alan had committed himself to helping me pass my A levels, a task which had assumed the level of a quest, he said I

188

should destroy all my racist literature. 'How can you understand Shakespeare, Chaucer, T.S. Eliot if you're limited by such things as race, class or religion? And having had a good look at Edna,' he added, 'I very much doubt she'd have passed one of the Führer's comb tests.'

It took some time before what he had said sank in. Then, like a couple of Mitfords, we roared with laughter as my mother entered the room. Jokingly, she told Alan, who was round at our house almost every night, that she'd love a photograph of him to put on the mantelpiece next to The Leader. But was she joking?

Alan was fascinated by the way she spoke. 'Especially when she talks about God. Have you noticed? She does the Jewish thing of talking direct to Him, as if He's with her in the room and has to answer her questions. Jews do that and so do Arabs. I can't think it's a form of address I've heard too often in the Church of England.'

'Alan,' my mother said, 'I've just come back from a house meeting in Notting Hill Gate.' The Leader had decided to talk to people in their houses all over Notting Hill Gate. It was a technique he had learnt during his early days with the Labour Party in the 1920s, when he'd been hailed as the Messiah of the New Left. 'Alan, I couldn't believe my eyes or my ears. There were about thirty people in the room, most of them Irishwomen. He spoke for almost two hours, mostly about the First World War, Lloyd George, and his friendship with Macmillan. Then he started talking about how he had opposed the Second World War and had met Hitler only twice and didn't really like him. How he got married in Berlin and kept it quiet in 1936 because he didn't want his second wife to be attacked by his opponents. He told these bored women that he'd loved his first wife very much but that she'd been victimised because of him. I thought all these women were falling asleep. Then,' my mother's eyes flashed, and Alan looked avidly on, busy putting her into his next novel, 'he recalled how he had read the Greeks when he was in prison with Lady Mosley and started talking about Socrates, Plato, Sophocles and Euripides. Suddenly, this huge woman at the back stood up. The Leader reacted as if he'd been shot, but kept quiet and let her speak. She said, "Sir Oswald, I don't know about your Greeks, but I've got niggers in the basement." '

Alan was helpless with laughter. His breath was coming in short gasps as he repeated her words, which would soon be reverberating around Le Temple de la Gloire, and into the ears of the best-known of the Mitford girls, authoress Nancy. 'I don't know about the Greeks, Sir Oswald, but *I've got niggers in my basement . . . !*' he shrieked.

Later, Alan sat with me in the Portman Arms and said that there must be some method in The Leader's madness. 'When he talks to Irish ladies with niggers in the basement he discusses Socrates, Sophocles, Euripides and Plato, and when he has an audience which includes half the Roman Catholic Church, Colin Wilson, and a reporter from *The Times*, he tells people about Lassie for dogs and Kitty Kat for wogs.'

That night, after a couple of pints and a lot of laughter, I knew that my days as a loyal supporter of Oswald Mosley had finally come to an end. He was no longer God; he could be laughed at. He wasn't going to lead anyone to a Promised Land; he didn't understand those he spoke to. But if I wasn't with the Movement, who was I with? I wished I could be back again with The Harlequins.

Despite the fact that I considered myself no longer 'with Mosley', I continued to attend meetings, partly out of curiosity, partly because I had no other social life.

The last night of Mosley's 1959 comeback campaign ended with him making a magnificent speech in Ladbroke Grove which revealed, once again, his amazing power as an orator of the grand style. He spoke about Europe, the need for unity and for a massive display of national will to save Britain from becoming a third-rate country, an appendage of America.

His speech was reasoned and reasonable. In it there was no reference to cat or dog foods or derogatory remarks about non-white immigrants. When he came down from his platform, Mosley was shining again. Had votes been counted there and then, he might have won. Fanatical supporters raised their right arms to salute him and

Mosley smiled and laughed, making them, daring them, to love him more. When he started his march back to his local headquarters, men on either side linked arms with him, all comrades together.

At first, I did not march alongside Mosley but on the pavement, to one side, as if I was not really a part of it, an observer rather than a participant, a camera recording a great event in my life but an event which signalled the end of something.

I saw Jeffrey and Bob smiling and laughing with Mosley and in that vital crowd were many faces I'd known since I was eight years old. They never seemed to change. But I knew, in my student donkey jacket and dark brown hair growing longer by the week, that I was different. I had changed. I was changing.

A boy in the crowd, shouted at me, 'Fuckin' journalist! You always get it wrong. What are you going to say about this in the morning, then?'

As the crowd progressed, it grew, until there were thousands of cheering, excited Mosley supporters. There was a joyful, party atmosphere. Mosley was ten feet tall again and shining like a knight. Everyone around him caught that glow and I soon found myself once more enveloped by the crowd. I was transported back to a time when, eight years old, a crowd had held me as the Horst Wessel song played and my father stood with his fist on his chest, my mother with her eyes closed, looking lost in prayer, and Lovene restless, not understanding my 'But, Beamie, this is the greatest night in the whole of history'.

A group of us crammed our way into the small headquarters, whilst outside hundreds of people chanted in the dark streets. The Leader looked at us with such pride in his face and he stood so tall and strong, showing his little, almost savage teeth, flashing his eyes as he heard again for the thousandth time:

> *Two, four, six, eight*
> *Who do we appreciate?*

And then everyone in the room and the street answering back with thunder in their voices:

191

'We've won,' he said. 'We've won.'

The following night, when the result was announced, I stood outside Kensington Town Hall. I was not an official so I could not get into the main room where the candidates were gathered. Mosley hadn't waited like this for an election result for thirty years.

Labour won, and Mosley came bottom of the poll with eight per cent, 2,811 votes. For the first time in his career, from the day he'd become a public figure and the 'baby' of the House in 1918, Mosley had lost his deposit.

I watched a blonde woman and her West Indian boyfriend jumping up and down outside the hall. 'He's come bottom!' she shouted. 'Mosley's come bottom.'

When he appeared from inside the hall, Mosley walked quickly to his car and gave a half-salute to his handful of followers. He got into the back and Jerry drove him away into the night.

I waited for John. He had a wife and a baby son, Vincent, to go home to. He was lucky. Most of the members had next to nothing in their lives apart from The Leader, who later admitted that the Notting Hill Gate defeat was the biggest single shock in his life.

We walked home in silence. When we reached Baker Street, I said to John, 'It's all over, John. I'm not going to waste any more time. I need to get some qualifications and I'm not going to spend time selling bloody *Union* newspapers in the street and screaming my lungs out for Oswald Mosley on a Saturday afternoon.'

John said he would think about his next move. He knew as well as I did that it was all over, and all that was left was the next punch-up, the next shout, the next defeat, which would be passed off as some sort of triumph.

When I told my mother and father, I knew that an era had ended.

'I told you Labour would win,' said my father.

'Maybe you could have done more, Trevor,' said my mother. 'You didn't speak once.'

'Mum,' I said, 'it's all over. It was over a long time ago.'

A week later, Jeffrey Hamm called a meeting at 302. Mosley was seated in a chair in the upstairs room. He said that he was taking a case to the High Court because there must have been some fiddling. So many canvassers who had recorded, at the least, a thirty per cent vote for him could not have been wrong. His decision was received in total silence.

The court case ended in defeat but Mosley didn't seem to mind. He came out of the High Court smiling and posed for photographers. He said to John, 'After that small setback we must move forward again.'

There is a picture of him taken at the Lido in Venice in 1962, after he had met with other aristocratic Fascist leaders and agreed to form a Continental party dedicated to the union of Europe. Considering his age and extraordinary life, he looked fit, even young and almost happy.

With the help of Alan Neame, I passed three A levels. The pictures in my room of Mosley, Hitler and Mussolini came down for good and books about skull sizes and nose shapes landed in the dustbin.

'And,' Alan said emphatically, 'if I'm your tutor, I insist you never open a book written by Kafka until you are at least thirty. If you did so now you would no doubt kill yourself.' But then he laughed.

I went to the City of London College in Moorgate as a part-time student and met a circle of people who introduced me to another world.

For a short time, I regularly saw a tall, intelligent and attractive St Albans' Art College student and took her to 40 Blandford Square to meet my mother. Afterwards, she said, 'Leave as soon as you can, Trevor. It's like a bunker. I felt as if a bomb was about to go off.'

Through Alan, I was introduced to the London editor of the Middle East News Agency. Both Alan and Desmond Stewart were highly respected writers in Egypt. The editor was a man called Mahmoud Amr who said he was surprised I knew so little about anything that was really happening in the world. I started, at the age of twenty-three, making him cups of tea and learning to use the telex.

After a year, I became MENA's correspondent in the House of Commons. Mr Amr said I might even make a good freelance reporter in the Middle East if I learnt Arabic. We became firm friends despite the difference in age and nationality. He lent me books about Islam, Zionism, the crusades and the rise of Arab nationalism. He was deeply anti-Israel and anti-Zionist but said sincerely that one could hate Zionism without being anti-Jewish.

Late one night in his office we sat drinking coffee and smoking endless cigarettes. After I had telexed the highlights of the British Sunday newspapers, he said, 'Trevor, as much as I like you and enjoy your company, you should try and get away from England. Your mother treats you like a little boy. She telephoned me last week to tell me she thinks your new girlfriend is involved with Christine Keeler and Mandy Rice Davies. I said, "Mrs Grundy, I've met the girl and she seems very nice" and she said, "Mr Amr, they all look nice as far as men are concerned. Will you tell Trevor you'll sack him unless he gets rid of her?"'

He looked at me with affection. 'You're twenty-five years old and your mother treats you like a child. That cannot be right. You must get away. Not just from Blandford Square, I mean a long, long way away. Perhaps Cairo . . . perhaps even further than Cairo.'

Towards the end of 1965, Michael Finlayson, a friend who worked as a reporter for an East End news agency, pushed a copy of the *UK Press Gazette* under the front door at 40 Blandford Square. A job advertisement was circled. It was for a sub-editor in a place called Ndola with *The Times of Zambia*.

I looked up Ndola on the map and it was in the Congo, which seemed romantic. Then I found the other Ndola on the Copperbelt in Zambia, which had been independent from Britain for exactly one year. A note with the paper said, 'This will get you out of the clutches of the you know whos.'

I applied for the job and was interviewed by the paper's editor in Fleet Street. Richard Hall told me that he wasn't looking for experts but did insist that his reporters and subs had no racial prejudices. I didn't get the job.

Two months later, I returned home in the early hours of the morning and found an air-mail letter under the door of the top-floor flat at 40 Blandford Square, which I now occupied. The man who'd been appointed to the job in Zambia had left for South Africa with a company car and not returned. How long would it take me to get to Ndola?

The weekend before my departure I walked with Nicholas Ashford, a friend who was to take over my job at the Middle East News Agency, round the famous abbey at St Albans. Nick showed me the walls and statues which had been desecrated by Cromwell's soldiers.

'I feel this is all mine,' he said. 'Don't you?'

'No,' I said from the bottom of my heart, and I really had no idea what he was talking about.

Soon after Easter 1966 I flew to Zambia via Uganda.

My mother and father, Lovene and her two sons, Vincent and Nicholas, took me to the airport. Lovene commented that I'd be away for three weeks or thirty years.

My father shook my hand and moved forward as if he was going to hug me, changed his mind and then stood back. He said, 'Be a man,' and then again, 'try to be a man.'

I kissed Lovene and put my arms around my mother. We said nothing. I never saw her again.

10

In Africa I felt free as I never had before. After one year I married a pretty eighteen-year-old born in Britain but brought up in Nigeria. I wrote and told my mother. She replied saying I was making a terrible mistake marrying a black.

'Don't be daft, Mum,' I wrote. 'Laurie was born in Liverpool.'

Her one-sentence reply read: 'Shirley Bassey was born in Cardiff.'

Towards the end of my two-year contract, I was offered a job in Julius Nyerere's 'Marxist' Tanzania. Before I left for Dar-es-Salaam, a letter came from my mother. It was full of sadness and regret about her life. She said that everyone had let her down, The Leader, my father, the rector, the man called Mr Lawes and me.

I replied with the sensitivity of an arrogant and inexperienced young man who had managed to re-create himself in Africa. I composed a letter which said no one had let her down, she had let herself down by being such a fanatic, by hating the Jews so much and making us believe in Mosley, who was an upper-class playboy who used people and then threw them away into, and I pompously used Lenin's famous phrase, 'the dustbin of history'.

I asked her if she had ever thought what being brought up as Fascists had done to Lovene and myself, how it had alienated us from our peer group? I dared her to tell me about her own childhood and why she was so pleased when people said she looked like a Jewess. I recalled the night in Notting Hill Gate when we had gone canvassing for Mosley and Mr Lewin had mistaken her for one.

My mother wrote back. She said that I was right. She had let herself down and blamed other people for her mistakes throughout her life. 'I've been a clown all my life,' she wrote. 'Don't be like your silly mother.' When I returned to England with my wife, she said, she would try to tell me about her strange childhood and answer my questions. But I left it too late.

In June 1970, three days before I was due to fly to Cairo on a sponsored trip, before returning to England for the first time in four years, I received a telephone call from Lovene in London. She told me that our mother, in the grip of another terrible depression, had committed suicide. She begged me to skip Cairo and fly straight to London.

'Come now. Right now. Please, Trevor. Please come now.'

For a reason I will never be able to explain, I went to Cairo with my wife Laurie and son Adam and kept to an itinerary drawn up by the Egyptian government. We toured Aswan, Luxor and Alexandria, the places my mother had always wanted to see.

I felt as though there was a bomb in my heart. 'How dare she?' I asked myself. 'How dare she kill herself on the eve of my return?' I had grown up. I had a wife and a son to prove it, but where was my mother to show all this off to?

Where is she? I cried out in my sleep. *Where is she?*

Back in London my father told me, 'She said to me the night before she killed herself, "Trevor will never see me like this, not like this with his new wife and son."' I felt as though I had killed her, the mother I hated more than anything on earth, whom I loved more than anything on earth, died because I was coming home.

Almost twenty years later, my father had a major heart attack and once more I was called urgently back to London by Lovene. 'I'm not doing it all on my own this time, Trevor. You've got to come.' Lovene was now living in California, where she worked at a Jesuit College. Like mine, her marriage had ended in divorce.

At the hospital, my father looked shrunken and weak. One of the nurses had been particularly kind to him, he told us. 'And would you believe it?' he whispered. 'A West Indian. Do you know what she did?'

We said no, as if we were talking to a child.

'She came in during her supper break with some pasta and sat right here by the bed. And I said to her, "Nurse," I said, "it's your supper break. What are you doing here, if I may so ask?"' He whispered more softly, as if he was confessing. 'She said to me, "Mr Grundy, I'd like to say some prayers by your bedside so that you'll get better." And I said, "Nurse, I've never been so touched in my life." And afterwards she stood up and just went away, eating her supper.'

A few days later he was well enough to return to his flat, where he lived with Peggy, my gentle Northumbrian stepmother. She was also my father's cousin and I had met her a few times as a child. She and my father had married in 1970, six months after my mother's suicide. My father sat in the living room watching television and became almost his old aggressive self. When the football results came on, he said, 'Do you know Sunderland's put a bloody nigger in the forward line?'

I wanted to get hold of the nurse's pasta and stick it up his nose.

'Your nurse last week, the one you liked so much, was a bloody nigger, or have you forgotten?'

He looked unembarrassed. 'Africa's done you no good. No good at all. You're like your sister now. She's in with the Catholics. A couple of lefties.'

The night before I left, he poured himself a large Scotch. 'Hang about, Dad,' I said. 'You've just had a heart attack and that would sink a battleship.'

Peggy was baking in the kitchen. He looked at the door to see if it was firmly shut and spoke softly to me. 'I always loved yer mam,' he said. 'She was wild but, my God, she was a fascinating woman.' He looked at the door again. 'When you left, she grew very old and tired and lost most of her glorious hair, Trevor. Sometimes she went days without saying a word. It was driving me crazy. It was no life. I used to come home after driving the cab all day and ask myself why I was still alive. It was only going up north and seeing Peggy that kept me going. Well, she is part of the family.'

He knocked back his drink almost savagely. 'I'm telling you this because I could go any time. I'm not stupid. Lovene knows about it, I think – about yer mam – but it's like everything else in this family. No one ever says anything.'

I sat down and watched him as he twiddled with the top of the bottle and then poured himself another but much smaller drink.

'A few days before she died, yer mam and I had a terrible row about something or other and I said that I'd tell you she was Jewish and she said, "Trevor will never know. He'll never know unless I tell him."'

'Did she really say that, Dad?' I asked, my heart thumping. 'Are you sure? Did she actually admit it and say, yes, I'm Jewish?'

'Yes. She *was* Jewish. Once, when we were courting, I went round to see yer mam at Whitley Bay. It was a Friday night and in their house all the lights were off and the front room was lit by candles. One of the neighbours said I should keep away from the Maurice family because they always did that on a Friday night and that they worshipped the devil and the council should give them the boot and make them live down in London where devil-worship didn't matter.

'When we were married, her mam used to boast that they could trace the family right back to the Jews in Spain. They hid their origins because people in England hate the Yids. They told Edna to hide her roots, to go for being a Christian, a gentile. Her old lady said she should never let anyone know what went on at the weekends. Home and outside were different worlds. Totally different places. Judaism was their secret. She never told anyone but me. Probably that Lawes man knew. Probably he knew more than anyone because she was so young and she'd have talked, I suppose. She called me by his name once and I thought I was going to kill her.'

He took another long drink from his glass. 'Do you remember, yer mam always wore a cross? She told me once that the old lady – yer grandma Maurice – used to say that as late as 1895 the Catholics in Spain were calling for a renewal of the Inquisition so they could prosecute the Jews – so hiding was second nature to them. Yer mam was brought up a Methodist to the outside world. All that hymn singing. She knew the lot. She loved that about the Movement, all the singing and the drums. And the secrecy, I suppose, the intrigue. It was what she was used to. God, how I hated the Maurices. She did too but she loved them at the same time . . .'

'Dad,' I said, glad at last to be getting some answers, 'why did you and Mum get involved with the Movement? I mean, didn't you see that Mosley was playing some sort of game, for whatever the reason? I mean, in a way he was worse than Hitler because at least Hitler believed in what he was doing. Mosley wasn't really anti-Jewish, was he? Mosley just used people. And you went to prison for that?'

'It was your mother. I only got involved with Mosley because of her. I told you, Jews are fanatics.' And then he added in a whisper, 'I think she was in love with him. He looked so Jewish himself. I think that was part of it.'

My father sat close to me and for a moment I thought he was going to hold my hand but he drew back, as he always had. 'I knew she was Jewish from the moment I met her but how could that stop the love?' Tears filled his watery, pale blue eyes.

'Dad,' I said. We looked at each other and I knew I'd never see him again.

He smiled and said, 'You've got your mother's eyes. Same way of looking.'

We heard the kettle whistle and sat up straight. He stood up and I heard his knees creak. He smiled. 'Old age – you can keep it.'

He turned down the music on the gramophone, the 'Venusberg' from *Tannhäuser*, and slid open the glass door of his bookshelf. He handed me his signed copy of Mosley's *The Alternative*. Then he gave me the German leather-bound book on Hitler. These were the books I had been promised if I stayed a good Fascist all my life.

He looked like so many Union Movement people who could neither love nor trust any more. 'When I'm dead I don't want there to be any memories. I want there to be nothing which showed I ever walked the earth. Do you understand? No memories.'

Epilogue

It was Friday and the following evening I would fly home to Africa. My father's funeral was over, Jane had gone to stay with her mother in Kent and I had a day to myself in London. It was the night of the Bethnal Green party and I could imagine the drums being taken down and dusted off.

I left Rayner's Lane and went by Underground to Baker Street. From there I walked to Regent's Park where springtime's ice still rimmed the edge of the lake. I walked around the Outer and Inner Circles and sat on the wall of the Louis XIV-style fountain in Queen Mary's Gardens, where my mother and I had walked Bonnie when I was small. I had a cup of tea and bought a packet of cigarettes. I walked to Marylebone Station, up Harewood Avenue and turned right into Blandford Square.

St Edward's Convent still stood, but opposite was only a row of neatly placed modern council houses. If I kicked a tennis ball over the convent wall, would a pretty Irish novice come to the front door grille and say, 'This is the last time I'm giving you your ball back today, you naughty boy'?

I turned into Lisson Grove and standing there like a long-forgotten friend was Christ Church, with its neo-classical façade, grey-white pillars and its blue-faced clock with gold numerals. I stood looking at the deconsecrated building and then went in through the front door.

I told the receptionist that I had attended this church as a boy and

201

asked if I could look around. She said it was now the headquarters of Aspel Communications. 'You'll find it's probably changed a bit,' she added.

I walked down what had been the aisle to the back of the building where we had changed into our white choir surplices or our full-length red server's cassocks. For a moment, the buzz of computers was replaced by the sound of an organ.

The modernisers hadn't changed too much. There was still an upstairs gallery which made the church, or office, look like a synagogue. The pulpit, where the rector and Mr Cooper had preached well or badly, according to what my mother thought that day, was no longer there, replaced by an instant coffee machine.

The organ had gone and so had the communion rail close to where I had sung in my still unbroken voice about a God who so loved the world that He made it possible for even the worst sinners to live again.

I looked up at Cave's fresco. I hadn't seen it since I was twelve, when my mother, rage and sorrow in her heart, had taken me away from this holy place.

I felt a hand on my arm. 'Are you all right? Would you like a cup of coffee?'

I walked with the girl to where the pulpit had been. 'Hope you don't mind instant.'

She was of West Indian extraction and had an open, kind face. Her sister might have been the nurse with the pasta. I told her I lived in Africa. She said that was funny because her grandfather came from Trinidad and she lived in Wimbledon.

I finished my coffee and stood up. I heard a voice singing and wondered if it was a record. But it was a boy's voice. It was loud and clear and it cut through the dark years which had followed my mother's death; black-cloud years which I felt descend on me so often. I heard it clearly because it was my voice.

> *O lamb of God*
> *That taketh away the sins of the world*
> *Have mercy upon us.*

O lamb of God
That taketh away the sins of the world
Grant us Thy peace.

I turned and looked at where the pews had been and saw a group of people moving towards the front of the church. They were staring at the altar and the large gold cross which stood upon it. Then one of them turned and, although I could not see her face clearly, she seemed to be smiling. She knelt down at the communion rail and put her hands out. She cupped them, right on top of left, to receive the Lamb of God which the prayer had urged her to take. I moved forward but the picture clouded and I again heard the low hum of computers.

I looked sideways at the fresco and said to the girl, 'I feel sorry for the disciples. I mean, there they are, fast asleep, it's cold and raining and they're told to get up and get going again.'

She laughed. 'I suppose that's all you can do, really, isn't it?'

I shook her hand and thanked her. I felt in my pocket to see if I had a business card. Who knows, one day she might fly to Zimbabwe to see the Victoria Falls. Instead I found the card James had given me at my father's funeral and for a brief moment I heard the sound of men marching and the rat-a-tat-tat of drums.

'Have you got a wastepaper basket?' I asked her. 'I need somewhere to put this.'

RUNNING WITH THE MOON

Jonny Bealby

Jonny Bealby was devastated when his fiancée, Melanie, died unexpectedly while they were travelling in Kashmir. Two years later and still heartbroken and utterly disillusioned, he took on the challenge of a lifetime. Setting off with only his motorbike for company, he began a daring and dangerous journey around the African continent in a desperate attempt to unearth some meaning in his life.

A true love story, *Running with the Moon* is a tale of great adventure and courage.

'Bealby handles this tragic tale with endearing honesty and tenderness. It is the romantic's naïvety, not to mention his irrepressible energy, optimism and courage, which . . . charm the reader'
Daily Telegraph

'Touching and honest'
Traveller

'An intriguing and . . . poignant record of one man's journey'
Impact

FINAL ROUNDS

James Dodson

James Dodson and his father had made themselves a promise: one day, before it was too late, they would travel together to Britain to play the great golf courses that Brax Dodson had played as an American airman during the Second World War. Finally they were ready to go. But Fate intervened and their trip took on a new urgency, an added poignancy: Brax was terminally ill, with only a few months to live.

Final Rounds is James Dodson's warm, moving and funny account of those precious last days they shared playing the game they loved and revealing not only the depth of their feelings for each other, but some of the secrets they had kept hidden for so long. *Final Rounds* is a great book about golf and its history and lore, and a wonderful book about the love of a father and a son for each other.

'This bittersweet book will fire an arrow through your heart . . . *Final Rounds* is the best'.
Sunday Times

'Good-humoured and overwhelmingly tender . . . With all the qualities of classic fiction, Dodson's wonderful book will teach you a lot about life, a little about golf, and have you wishing for even a quarter of the relationship he obviously had with his father. Heartbreaking.'
Maxim

NO CAKE, NO JAM

Marian Hughes

Condemned to a life of harsh discipline in a south London oprhanage, Marian Hughes spent her childhood dominated by the Bible, extravagant hymns and regular beatings.

Then, when Marian was ten, her mother reclaimed her. But life with mother was no easier, as the family moved from one dirty flat to another. Left to fend for herself in wartime London, Marian learned the hard way about stealing, begging and avoiding the authorities.

Worse, she gradually learned that her frequently violent mother was in fact seriously deranged. Despite this, Marian never lost her spirit or faltered in her loyalty. *No Cake, No Jam* is the heart-warming story of a girl who rose above adversity through sheer guts and strength of character.

ARROW ORDER FORM